Start Beginning:

Christian Basics for Faith and Life

Revised and Updated Edition

To Ted:

Thank you for so many things!

Tim

PRAISE FOR 'STARTING AT THE BEGINNING'

"If there is someone in your life who you would like to introduce to Jesus, this book will help you do so. Buy two copies and give one to your friend. Then, meet with them weekly to read it through chapter by chapter, as you explore together what it means to become a Christian and then live as a follower of Jesus. The sound biblical and theological teaching it offers is shared in language people today will understand. The personal anecdotes, metaphors, and examples peppered across its pages will help bring these teachings further to life. It is simply a wonderful gift, both to those wanting to share the Christian faith and to those wanting to explore it."

Judy Paulsen
Professor of Evangelism,
Wycliffe College, Toronto

"The call of Jesus to follow him includes every aspect of our lives. In his book *Starting at the Beginning,* Tim Chesterton calls new and old believers alike to allow this call to permeate every aspect of their thinking, living, and relating. Accessible to new believers with enough meat for long time followers, this book will help Christians from every tradition grapple with what it means to follow Jesus in an integrated way."

Daren Wride
Author, *DNA of a Christ Follower*

Starting at the Beginning:

Christian Basics for Faith and Life

Revised and Updated Edition

Tim Chesterton

Foreword by

Bishop Stephen London

ISBN: 978-1-7389231-0-6

For Jamie, Corinna, Jenny, Mary-Lou, and Doreen

'In all my prayers for all of you, I always pray with joy because of your partnership in the gospel from the first day until now.'

(Philippians 1.4-5 NIV)

TABLE OF CONTENTS

FOREWORD

STEPHEN LONDON, ANGLICAN BISHOP OF EDMONTON

I have known Tim Chesterton for a long time, and I love to hear him speak as well as play guitar. He has a great gift for telling stories and getting to the heart of important matters. And in this book, he does both. *Starting at the Beginning* is written for people like you who are exploring and asking questions about Christian faith. This book is a very good place to start.

But it was also a gift to me. I have been a follower of Jesus for many years now, and as I read this book I was encouraged again and again. What I love the most about it, is that Tim has painted such a generous vision of the Christian faith. It is a vision that is both faithful to the New Testament witness and profoundly relevant for the questions we are asking in the 21st century. It reminded me again of why I love this way of life so much.

Starting at the Beginning will help you ask the big questions about who Jesus is, and it is also practical about what a relationship with Jesus looks like from day to day. Tim articulates well what Christians believe, but also gives space for you to ask your questions. Whether you are reading this book by yourself, or as part of a group asking questions together, I encourage you not to rush through it. Read it with both your mind and your heart. God speaks to both. And I pray that you truly find what you are looking for.

INTRODUCTION

A VERY GOOD PLACE TO START

The first time I tried to read *The Lord of the Rings,* I only made it through about thirty pages, and then I gave up.

This might come as a surprise to some of my friends, who know how much I love that book (and all the works of J.R.R. Tolkien, actually). I'm such a committed *Lord of the Rings* fan that when the Peter Jackson movie adaptations first came out, my children were nervous about going to see them with me; they were afraid I was going to make disparaging comments out loud in the theatre! I didn't, but I have to admit that to this day, if I hear someone begin a sentence with, "As Gandalf says…," my ears immediately prick up: are they about to quote a *genuine* Gandalf saying, from the book, or a fake one, from the movies?

So how was it that a committed *Lord of the Rings* geek like me had a bad experience with the book the first time he tried to read it? The answer is simple: I didn't start at the beginning.

I'd actually come across the *Lord of the Rings* for the first time in an anthology I was required to read as part of my high school English class. I think I was about fifteen at the time, and I had never heard of Tolkien or any of his works. But the extract in the anthology was particularly vivid, and I knew right away that I wanted to read this book. So I put a hold on it at the local library (that was when I discovered it had been published in three volumes), and the first volume to arrive was *The Two Towers,* which is actually the second book in the series, not the first.

Tolkien did his best; he included a short summary of the plot of book one, *The Fellowship of the Ring,* at the beginning of the second volume. But it wasn't enough. I wasn't familiar with the characters, I didn't really know what elves and hobbits and orcs were, and I had only a very basic understanding of why the Ring was so powerful and important. As I said, I got about thirty pages in and then gave up. I couldn't really enjoy book two without first reading book one.

"Let's start at the very beginning; it's a very good place to start." This well-known quote from the old movie *The Sound of Music* is good advice for many situations in life. In most cases, it's really hard to jump into a subject halfway through. Universities aren't being mean when they insist that you take the 101-level course before proceeding to the higher levels. They do that for our benefit!

This is definitely true of Christianity. You might be a long time Christian, or a brand-new believer; you might not be sure you are a believer—or you might be absolutely sure you're not! You may have been a church member for years, or you may never have darkened the doors of a church. Whatever your current situation, you're going to find it easier to grasp the big picture of Christianity if you start at the beginning.

~

Just a quick word about where this book came from. When it was originally published in 2004, it had grown out of a Christian Basics course I'd been teaching for several years. Over time the course had evolved, but the aim had always been the same: to communicate the Christian faith in a helpful way for people who were on their way into it, or at least were contemplating the journey.

The book was a snapshot of my thinking when it was written, but since then, I've continued to grow and learn, and our society has evolved as well. The original book is long since out of print, and I've felt for a while that a revised edition would be useful. The Covid-19 pandemic gave me the opportunity; our parish held a 'Starting at the Beginning' course on Zoom, and I did some substantial work on revising and updating the talks for that course. Now, two years later, they've been expanded into the chapters of the book you're holding in your hands.

I have no way of knowing why you've decided to read this book. You might be an inquirer—someone who makes no claim to be a Christian but is interested in learning what Christianity is all about. You might be a new Christian who feels the need for a more secure grounding in the basics of your faith. You might be a long-time churchgoer who has realized that, although you've been part of the church for years, you've never discovered a living connection with Jesus. Or you might be a faithful, lifelong Christian who senses the need to go back to the basics so you can rediscover the joy of the gospel for yourself.

Whatever your situation might be, I hope you'll find two things in this book.

First, I hope you'll find the information you need to make an intelligent decision about Christianity—or, if you've already made that decision, to give it a strong foundation in basic Christian teaching. Nicky Gumbel, the face behind the *Alpha* course, tells of someone coming up to him one evening about halfway through a course and saying, "I've finally realised what you're doing. It's like a jigsaw puzzle; each night we're being given another one of the pieces, and I've just started to glimpse the picture." I hope that as you go through this book you'll start to glimpse the big picture of what a life of faith in Jesus is all about.

That leads to the second thing I hope you'll discover. Most of us know there's more to life than being alive in the biological sense. Sometimes we even say to our friends, "Get a life!" We know it's possible to live out the days of our biological life without being fully alive, without discovering and experiencing what life is really all about.

The early Christians knew this too. One of them, the writer of the Gospel of John, has this to say near the end of his book:

> 'Now Jesus did many other signs in the presence of his disciples that are not written in this book. But these are written so that you may continue to believe that Jesus is the Messiah, the Son of God, and that through believing you may have life in his name.' (John 20:30-31)

In other words, John didn't want to limit himself to conveying information; he wanted to help his readers discover life in all its fulness. He believed this life could be found in a relationship with the living God who has been made known to us in Jesus. That may or may not be your belief as you start this book, but I'm sure you'll agree that the question is a crucial one. As Harold Percy has said, there are some people whose epitaph at the end of their lives might be 'Brilliant performance, but they missed the whole point.' None of us wants to be in that situation. If there's a way to 'get a life' in the fullest possible sense, then the important thing is to find it. If this book helps some people to find that life, in relationship with the God who is revealed to us in Jesus, then it will have accomplished its purpose.

~

The Structure of this Book

As I mentioned, this book began its life as a series of talks I developed for a course for inquirers. The course was divided into two parts: 'Christian Basics' (four sessions), and 'Growing and Living as a Christian' (six sessions). Not everyone who took the first part went on to part two, so there needed to be some overlap.

Chapter Four, 'Where Do I Go From Here?', was the overlap; it gave a bird's-eye view of what came next. Much of the material in this chapter is developed in greater detail in chapters five to eight, while chapters nine and ten are entirely new.

I have preserved that structure in this book, because some people may wish to use this material as the basis for two courses, as it was originally designed. This means that there is some duplication between chapter four and the chapters that follow, but I hope that the further development in chapters five to eight will make it worthwhile.

~

Sources

The original material in the 'Christian Basics' course was not my own; it came from Harold Percy, who was then the rector of Trinity Church, Streetsville, Ontario. I first received it from

Harold in the 1990s; over the years since then I've adapted it, deleting and adding as it seemed right, to the point that it now bears very little resemblance to Harold's original! Nevertheless, it's still true that Harold was the inspiration behind this book and I'm glad to acknowledge my debt to him at the outset. Some of the additional material was my own, and some I found in other writers, including especially John Bowen, Nicky Gumbel, C.S. Lewis, William McKay, W.H. Griffith Thomas, Rico Tice, Francis Spufford, N.T. Wright, and Philip Yancey. At the end of each chapter I have tried to give accurate credit to my original sources.

Nicky Gumbel's 'jigsaw puzzle' quote comes from the training videos for leaders of the *Alpha* course.

I heard Harold Percy's quote "Brilliant performance..." in the context of one of his many excellent workshops on evangelism and congregational development.

CHAPTER 1:

HOW CAN I UNDERSTAND GOD'S STORY IN THE BIBLE?

I was born in 1958, just thirteen years after the end of the Second World War. Both my parents had lived through the war, and war stories and war movies were common on TV when I was a child. Those stories continued to have a powerful effect on those of us in the succeeding generation.

I think, for instance, of the tale of the Battle of Britain. The way it was commonly told, Germany had this enormous air force (the Luftwaffe), with thousands of bombers and fighters sent over every day to attack Britain. To protect us (notice how I learned to use the word 'us', even though I hadn't been around at the time), we in Britain had a tiny Royal Air Force: a few hundred Spitfires and Hurricanes, flown by brave pilots who took off again and again through that summer of 1940, going fearlessly into battle to protect the helpless people below. Many gave their lives to save us, and their bravery won the day. The Spitfires and Hurricanes were better than anything the Luftwaffe had to throw at us, and so Hitler's plan to invade Britain was thwarted. As Winston Churchill put it, 'Never in the field of human conflict was so much owed by so many to so few.'

That was the way the story was told. I heard it many times, in many different formats. But I didn't realize until much later how the story was *forming* me.

It was teaching me to be proud of being British. The Germans were trying to conquer the world; they had defeated everyone else in Europe, and only we British stood between them and world dominion. This is what we do, we Brits: we fight for freedom (notice how the story of our colonial past was glossed over in this narrative).

It was teaching me to hate Germans. In many of the books I read, Germans were cruel and heartless; all they seemed to care about was torturing and killing people who were not German. Of course, I hadn't met any Germans at the time, so I had no personal experience to go by. It took many years for me to learn a world view in which Germans weren't automatically the villains.

It was teaching me to root for the underdog. In the fight between David and Goliath, I was definitely on the side of David. The Royal Air Force was small, and the Luftwaffe was big, but that didn't matter; right was on our side (note how I used that word 'our' again), so we won.

This is the power of a story. It tells you who you are, and who your enemies are. It tells you what you value and what isn't important. It tells you what success looks like. It tells you who you can trust and who you should be wary of.

Many years later, as an adult, I came to understand that the story of the Battle of Britain had become part of our British national mythology. When I use the word 'mythology', I don't necessarily mean it was untrue (although I now know there were many inaccuracies in the way the story was commonly told). I mean that for us, it wasn't just a story; it was a parable, a folk tale, a defining moment in our national life. And I had no problem reading myself into that story. I was one of 'us', the brave generation that fought that battle, even though I hadn't been born yet. In some mysterious way, even though the story was in the past, it was still present to those of us who heard it. It was 'our' story.

~

I would argue that most nations have significant stories that have shaped their national lives. For the United States, I think of the War of Independence (and, for some, the Civil War). For France, it might be the storming of the Bastille. For modern Jewish people, the story of the Holocaust has had a profound impact.

But I've noticed in recent years that new generations are seeking new stories, and they sometimes find them in strange places. Back in the 1970s there was a bumper sticker that proclaimed, 'Gandalf for President!' Gandalf, of course, is a fictional character in J.R.R. Tolkien's great book *The Lord of the Rings.* He never lived, but millions of people around the world have gotten to know him through the book (or the movies based on the book), and many have come to admire him for his wisdom and courage. Star Trek fans often see Captain Jean-Luc Picard (of *Star Trek: The Next Generation*) in a similar light. In fact, I've been amazed at how thoroughly many people have inhabited the Star Trek universe; it has shaped their values and the way they see the world. In the fullest possible sense, they have been *formed* by it.

What do I mean by 'formed'? I mean that these stories define our ideals for us, and they motivate us to reach toward them. They help us find answers to the fundamental questions of life. "Why am I here?" "What am I supposed to do with my life?" "How do I know what's right and what's wrong?" "Where is it all going to end?" I've heard these questions described as 'God-shaped questions', because Christians believe there's no way of answering them adequately without including God in our answer.

What do we even mean by the word 'God'? Christians, like their Jewish ancestors in the faith, have always answered that question by telling a story. If you had asked an Israelite in the eight century BCE, "Which god do you believe in?" the response would probably have been something like, "I believe in the God who rescued us from our slavery in Egypt" (note, again, how the person answering that question would use the word 'us', even though the events in the story had happened long before they were born). If you had asked the same question of a Christian in the first century AD, the response might well have been, "I believe in the God who raised Jesus from the dead." The story they were referring to told them about their god, but it also told them about themselves and their place in the world. I think that, deep down inside, all of us are looking for a story like that.

~

Like many people of my generation, I grew up in a home where the Christian story was known and loved. My parents took me to church on Sundays, and at home they read me Bible stories and prayed with me. When I was a little boy, my dad went away to seminary to train to be a minister, and on one of his holidays he brought home a Bible story book for my brother and me. It had lots of wonderful water-colour illustrations, and I loved leafing through the pages, looking at all the pictures of Moses and Elijah and Jesus and Paul and all the rest. I was enjoying those pictures long before I learned to read the book.

And so I grew up knowing lots of Bible stories: Adam and Eve, Noah and the Ark, Moses leading the people through the Red Sea, David and Goliath, the birth of Jesus, the feeding of the five thousand, the death and resurrection of Jesus—to name just a few. But I wasn't so familiar with the 'big story' of the Bible and how the individual stories fit into it. Or, to put it another way, I didn't know that *the Bible itself is a story*. It has a beginning and an end, and a plan for getting from one to the other. It has a plot outline. It has heroes and villains, conflict and resolution, tension and disaster, and characters who grow and learn.

For those of us who grow up in Christian households, learning about this story is one of the main ways we learn about God. We don't usually start off by memorizing the Nicene Creed or the statements of belief put out by various Christian churches. We start off by hearing the story. After we've been listening to it for a few years, we discover that we actually know quite a lot about who God is and what God is like. But our learning didn't come from memorizing intellectual propositions; it came from watching God at work in the pages of the Bible.

Of course, not everyone gets it. Some children grow up in Christian homes but somehow don't see the big picture of what God is doing. Some of them decide later in life that Christianity is not for them. And many people have had no exposure to Christianity beyond what they see in popular media. Through no fault of their own, they wouldn't be able to tell you much about the Christian story.

This book is called 'Starting at the Beginning', so this is where I want to start. I want to spend this first chapter giving you an overview of the story the Bible tells. Once we get this overview firmly into our minds, we'll be in a better position to see how the individual stories fit into it. And I'd like to suggest that it can be helpful to see the Bible as something like a play with six acts.

~

Act 1: Creation

In this act, God created the universe and everything in it, including this earth on which we live. As the book of Genesis puts it, 'In the beginning God created the heavens and the earth' (Genesis 1:1 NIV).

Of course, we now have a much bigger view of what creation entailed. We know about the untold millions of years during which God was slowly shaping the evolution of life on this planet, preparing it for the arrival of humankind. In years gone by, many Christians were afraid of this evolutionary story; they saw it as a competitor to the biblical account of creation. But nowadays most Christians believe these two accounts don't contradict each other; they're simply different kinds of literature, answering different kinds of questions.

What were the authors of the Bible trying to teach us in their creation stories?

First, *they believed that the world is the good creation of a good God.* Over and over again, in the first chapter of Genesis, we're told that after creating something, 'God saw that it was good.' The God of the Hebrew scriptures is curiously uninterested in some unseen 'spiritual' world; God is interested in oceans and mountains, rivers and valleys, birds and fish and animals—and people. 'God saw everything that he had made, and indeed, it was very good' (Genesis 1.31).

Second, *they believed that this world still belongs to God,* because God made it and has never given it away to anyone else. One of their hymn writers described it like this:

> The earth is the Lord's and all that is in it,
> the world, and those who live in it;

> for he has founded it on the seas,
> and established it on the rivers. (Psalm 24.1-2)

True, God has entrusted the earth to human beings as stewards of creation, but it's not our possession. We're tenants; we're not owners, and we shouldn't treat the earth as if it was our property.

Third, *they believed that human beings are created in the image of God,* as the Bible says in Genesis 1.27.

Obviously, this wasn't meant to suggest that we resemble God in a physical sense. There have been many suggestions down through the years as to what 'being made in the image of God' actually means, but I suggest that, at heart, it's a parental metaphor. The same phrase is used in Genesis 5 to describe Adam's son Seth: '...Adam...became the father of a son in his likeness, according to his image, and named him Seth' (Genesis 5.3). Sometimes we say of a child that 'she's the spitting image of her mother.' But there are other ways in which children often resemble their parents: personality, temperament, speech patterns, values. As human beings made in God's image, we're created to learn God's vision and values. That's what it means to be made in the image of God.

Fourth, although they generally used male imagery for God, *they certainly didn't believe that God was an exclusively male god.* Note carefully:

> 'So God created humans in his image,
> in the image of God he created them;
> *male and female* he created them' (Genesis 1.27, emphasis mine)

So both male and female express the image of God.

Fifth, the authors of Genesis believed that *we are the stewards of God's creation.* God is certainly up to the job of caring for the earth without our help, but God chose to involve us in that project. We've been placed on this planet as God's representatives, to care for God's creation and protect it from harm. This is the meaning behind the symbolic language of Genesis: 'The Lord

God took the man and put him in the garden of Eden to work it and take care of it' (Genesis 2.15 NIV). So the good care of creation isn't just a trendy idea created by twenty-first century tree huggers. It's part of God's original call to us as human beings made in God's image.

Sixth, the authors of Genesis paint a picture of *a world of harmony and peace*. Genesis 3.8 talks about the Lord God 'walking in the garden at the time of the evening breeze.' Obviously this is mythological language, but it's clearly meant to describe a world in an idyllic state. Perhaps there was such a time, or perhaps the story is merely pointing us to God's ideal for us. I'm not sure myself which of those interpretations is right, but I'm not worried about it; either way, the story still stands as a powerful vision of God's dream for creation.

~

Act 2: Rebellion

God decided to give human beings the terrifying gift of free will. We can understand why God would do that. If we created an android and programmed it to love us, it might be enjoyable for us at first, but eventually it would seem rather hollow; we'd know our android had no choice in the matter. And in the same way, if God had simply created human beings with no choice about whether or not they would love God, their love wouldn't be real, because real love demands freedom of choice.

In Genesis chapter 3 we read about how the first human beings were tempted by a snake—an obvious symbol for the forces of evil—to step outside God's will for them and choose their own road instead. They were told that if they did this '...your eyes will be opened, and you will be like God, knowing good and evil' (Genesis 3:5). They gave in to this temptation to try to be gods for themselves, and as a result, evil and brokenness entered their lives for the first time.

It wasn't only their connection with God that was damaged; their relationships with each other and with the world around them were also disrupted. They were evicted from their beautiful garden home, a symbolic way of saying that paradise was lost to them as a result of their choice to rebel against God. And their sin had an effect on the natural world as well; God said to them "...cursed is the ground because of you; in toil you shall eat of it all the days of your life; thorns and thistles it shall bring forth for you..." (Genesis 3:17-18).

You'll notice that I'm interpreting this story as a symbolic account. It's meant to teach us that the world as we see it is not the world as God intended it to be. It's been infected by evil. This evil isn't just a force external to human beings; it's in each of us as well, in our hearts. Jesus said, "What comes out of a person is what defiles them. For it is from within, out of a person's heart, that evil thoughts come—sexual immorality, theft, murder, adultery, greed, malice, deceit, lewdness, envy, slander, arrogance and folly. All these evils come from inside and defile a person" (Mark 7:20-23, NIV).

My favourite way of summing up what we learn in Acts One and Two is in an unforgettable scene from an old movie, 'Good Morning, Vietnam'. The soundtrack for the scene is Louis Armstrong's famous song, 'What a Wonderful World'. The song paints a lovely picture of green trees and red roses, blue skies with white clouds, and friends shaking hands. But in the movie, the song says one thing and the pictures say another. They are pictures of war in Vietnam. As we're told that the roses 'bloom for me and you,' we see a child in the foreground and a bomb going off in the background. As we hear the words 'the colours of the rainbow so pretty in the sky,' we see protesters being beaten up and a young man being shot. And the chorus 'I say to myself, what a wonderful world' is accompanied by images of the bloodied sandal of a little child.

This is the world as we know it. It was made by a good and loving God and still contains many signs of God's goodness and love. Yet we know it's also infested with evil and sin. Evil has infected God's good creation and spoiled God's beautiful plan for the world. Instead of binding the world together, the loudest voices are often those of self-centredness and anger.

And we're all implicated in that. We human beings are capable of acts of immense kindness and compassion, and there are countless stories demonstrating that fact. But if we're honest, every single one of us is also well aware of what Francis Spufford calls our 'Human Propensity to Mess Things Up' (he actually uses a stronger word than 'mess', but 'mess' will serve for our purposes!). I know the truth of this from my own experience. Yes, I hunger for justice and goodness in my own life, but I also seem to have an amazing capacity for damaging things—and, worse, for damaging people. I know many others who feel the same way. When I ask people if they are sinners, they often say, "No, of course not!" But when I rephrase the question—when I ask, "Have you noticed that you have a real talent for messing things up?"—then the response is often quite different.

We live in a good world which has been spoiled by the power of evil and sin. But the good news is that God has not given up on creation. God intends to deliver it from its captivity to evil. Let's go on to Act 3.

~

Act 3: Israel

I began to learn to play guitar by myself with the help of an instruction book. This book taught me some basic chords and techniques, but my progress was slow and difficult. A little later, I met some more experienced guitarists and was able to watch and listen to them. They were my models, and by imitating them I was able to make much better progress.

God has always wanted a community of people who would learn a different way of living, and model it for the world around them. This is why, at the beginning of Act 3, God chose one elderly couple, Abraham and Sarah, calling them to leave their family and go to a new land. God promised to bless them and make their name great; in them God would bless all the families of the earth (see Genesis 12:1-3). Although they were too old to have children, God gave them a miracle child, Isaac. Isaac became the father of Jacob, and Jacob became the father of twelve sons who were the ancestors of the twelve tribes of Israel.

The story goes on to tell us how, many years later, God led those tribes out of slavery in Egypt and back to their own land, which later became known as 'Israel.' Through all the hundreds of years that followed, God was patiently teaching them.

They gradually came to understand that there was only one true God, and that idols were not real. They learned that God was the Creator of everything, and therefore all of creation belonged to God. They learned that God was holy and good, and wanted them to live lives of goodness and holiness. God gave them commandments to show them the kind of life that would be a blessing to the world around them.

The people struggled to learn these lessons, and the Hebrew scriptures—often called the Old Testament—tell the story of that struggle. The people in those old stories were far from perfect; they had the same weaknesses and sins and fears and temptations as us. At times we're caught up in the beauty of their vision of God; at other times we're appalled by their savagery and puzzled by their continued attraction to idols (not recognizing, of course, that we have false gods of our own that attract us in the same way).

As the story progressed, the people became a nation, and the nation became a monarchy. David wasn't its first king, but later generations looked back on him as their greatest ruler. He was a shepherd boy who became the leader of God's people, and in his story they found one of their most powerful images for God: 'The Lord is my shepherd, I shall not want' (Psalm 23.1). But after the death of David's son Solomon the kingdom was caught up in a civil war and split into two: 'Israel' (the northern tribes), and 'Judah' (the tribe of David, which remained faithful to his dynasty and his capital city of Jerusalem).

These two nations had the misfortune of sitting on a major trade route between several superpowers: Egypt, Philistia, Assyria, and Babylon. Their kings got caught up in the struggles between those superpowers, and the people often suffered as a result. Their prophets warned them that if they continued to rebel against God, they would eventually fall to their enemies, and in the end, that's what happened. In 722 BCE Israel fell to the Assyrians, and in 587 BCE Judah was conquered by the Babylonians. In each case, the educated people were taken away into captivity (since they were the ones who wrote the books, we can easily get the impression that the whole nation was deported, but in fact that wasn't the case).

In 538 BCE the exiles were given permission to return home from Babylon; some of them did, and over the next century they gradually rebuilt their life in their ancestral homeland. We can imagine how much they'd longed to go back to their own country, but when they returned home, the reality wasn't as idyllic as they'd hoped. Their physical exile had ended, but was there, perhaps, a more important exile, an estrangement from God, that still needed to be healed?

~

Act 4: Jesus

Typically, a novelist starts on a new story with some kind of plan in mind, but often, in the process of writing, the characters run away with the plot and start behaving in ways the author hadn't intended. This is what happened to God's world. And perhaps there was only one way for the divine author to bring the story back to its original purpose. Perhaps God needed to enter the story as one of the characters, and actually meet the other characters on their level, talk with them, and invite them back to the original plan.

Incredible though it may sound, that's what God did. In Act 4 God stepped onto the stage as one of the characters in the story: Jesus of Nazareth. And if the Creator of the universe has actually visited this planet in Jesus, then surely the story of Jesus' life, death and resurrection has to be the most important story ever told in human history.

We find the story of Jesus in the biblical documents we call the four gospels. They tell of how Jesus was born in unusual circumstances in Bethlehem and grew up in Nazareth near the Lake of Galilee. At the age of thirty he left his home and began a travelling ministry of preaching, teaching, and healing. The basic theme of his teaching was 'The Kingdom of God is at hand,' which meant that the time had come when God's kingly rule was going to be extended over this broken and spoiled world. God was going to defeat evil and restore creation to its original purpose. Jesus believed this was happening through his ministry.

Early in his ministry Jesus began to gather apprentices who could carry on his work; traditionally we've called them 'disciples' or 'apostles'. A lot of the material in the gospel accounts probably comes from them. In those days Jewish rabbis often taught their disciples by making them memorize their teaching, and there's no reason to believe Jesus was any different. Gradually, as these apprentices progressed in their training, Jesus sent them out on preaching and healing missions of their own.

But Jesus also aroused considerable opposition from the religious establishment, and this led to the most shocking part of the whole story. In the third year of his ministry Jesus was arrested in Jerusalem, given a mock trial before the ruling council of Israel, and handed over to the Romans, who executed him by crucifixion. This presented a problem for his followers. They had believed him to be the 'Messiah', a king like old King David, who would set Israel free and bring in God's kingdom of justice and peace. But would God have let the Messiah be arrested and executed? That was definitely not the way they had read the old prophecies!

However, on the third day after Jesus' death, strange things began to happen. Some of the women went to his tomb and found it empty. His followers began to see him alive again. He met with them over the next six weeks and taught them the true significance of what had happened. Gradually, as they looked back and reflected on all this, they came to understand that, through his death and resurrection, Jesus had somehow healed the great breach between God and humanity; he had brought the whole world home from its spiritual exile. And the New Testament goes on to tell us how, before he ascended into heaven, Jesus sent out his first apprentices to spread the story to others and invite them to be a part of it as well. And so, the church was born.

We're going to skip Act 5 for a minute and go on to Act 6...

~

Act 6: The End

Act 6 tells us that the story, like every good story, will have a definite ending. When the Bible tries to describe this ending, it uses highly symbolic language, and it can be difficult sometimes to work out exactly what the authors are trying to tell us. But the bare bones of the plot of Act 6 are that, at the end of the story, Jesus will come again as judge of the living and the dead, evil will be eradicated from the earth, and God's good and loving purposes for creation will finally be accomplished.

Notice that this isn't the ending we often hear about in popular spiritually. Many people in the world today think Christianity is all about knowing you're going to go to heaven when you die, but the people who wrote the books of the Bible had a much bigger hope. They believed the saving work of Jesus was going to transform the whole world. They believed the day would come when God's will would be done on earth as it is in heaven; that life on earth would be restored to the dream God had when God created the universe in the first place. This beautiful world that God took such care to create is not going to be set aside. God isn't going to abandon matter in favour of some higher, non-material reality. No—God loves this world of colour and music and scent and the joy of physical touch. One of the writers of the New Testament put it like this:

> 'For the creation was subjected to frustration, not by its own choice, but by the will of the one who subjected it, in hope that the creation itself will be liberated from its bondage to decay and brought into the freedom and glory of the children of God' (Romans 8.20-21 NIV).

~

Act 5: The Act that is still being written

We've reviewed the story the Bible tells us, from the moment of creation as far as the life of Jesus and the beginnings of the early church—Acts 1 to 4—and we've looked ahead to the conclusion of the tale—Act 6. Now it's time to get back to Act 5. The reason I missed it out is that *Act 5 is still being written!*

Tom Wright illustrates it like this. Suppose a previously unknown play by Shakespeare was discovered, but with one act missing. What could you do? He suggests you could gather together the world's most experienced Shakespearean actors, get them to read Acts 1-4 and Act 6 until the play is second nature to them, and then get them to improvise the missing act. If they're going to do a good job of it, they'll need to be true to Acts 1-4, and connect with the start of Act 6.

That's where we are in relation to the Christian story. God has given us a framework for our lives in Acts 1-4 and Act 6. All the clues for how to work out Act 5 are right there. It's as if God is saying to us, "Do you want to play a part in my story? I'd love it if you would!"

I note two things missing from Tom Wright's illustration. First, we're not the world's best Shakespearean actors. We're just ordinary fallible human beings! However, if we're worried about this, all we have to do is look back to Act 4 and see the kind of people Jesus chose to be his actors in that part of the story. They weren't experts either. Nonetheless, Jesus was able to teach them their parts, and when he sent them out to carry on the story, they did quite well!

The reason they did quite well has to do with the other thing Tom Wright left out of his illustration. There's no way the spirit of Shakespeare himself could somehow come and live in those actors and guide them as they perform their play. But the Christian story assures us that the Spirit of God can and does come and live in us apprentices of Jesus. And because of that, when we play our parts and say our lines, we're not limited to our own strength and wisdom. We have the power and wisdom of God living in us, to help us along the way.

This is the Christian story. As we've seen, it's not just a completed story from long ago. It's a story that still continues, and in which each of us is invited to play a part. God wants you and me to be part of this story. As this book continues, we'll find out how that can happen for each one of us.

~

Sources

The insight about Christians and Jews describing their God by means of stories comes from the early chapters of N.T. Wright's book *The New Testament and the People of God* (Minneapolis; Fortress Press; 1992).

The concept of 'God-shaped questions' comes from William J. McKay: *Me, an Evangelist?* (St. Louis; Stephen Ministries; 1992) 119ff.

The idea of the Christian story as a play in six acts is a modification of an idea by Tom Wright (*The New Testament and the People of God*, 140-141), further developed by Richard Middleton and Brian Walsh, *Truth is Stranger than it Used to Be*, (Downers Grove; InterVarsity Press; 1995), 182, 240.

The song 'What a Wonderful World' was written by George Weiss and Bob Thiele. Rico Tice uses it as an illustration of how the world is a combination of good and evil in his book *Christianity Explored: The Handbook* (Carlisle; Paternoster Publishing; 2001), 117.

Our 'human propensity to mess things up' is a phrase adapted from one used by Francis Spufford in his excellent book *Unapologetic* (London; Faber and Faber; 2012).

The illustration of an author writing himself into his own story is found in Sheldon Vanauken: *A Severe Mercy* (New York; Harper and Row/Bantam Books; 1977, 1979), 113-114.

CHAPTER 2:

WHERE DOES JESUS FIT IN?

Why is Jesus important? That's the next question we have to consider. Why are we Christians not satisfied with just believing in God? After all, many people are attracted to the idea that there is a wise and loving God who created everything that exists. Why do we have to be any more specific than that? Why do we want to tie ourselves down to the life, death and reported resurrection of an obscure Galilean carpenter who lived two thousand years ago? What's so special about him?

That's a fair question, and I want to answer it in three parts. I believe we should consider Jesus because of his life, his death, and his resurrection.

~

Jesus' life

The gospels tell us very little about the early life of Jesus. Like many other young men in those days, he seems to have learned his trade from his father, the village carpenter. But when he was about thirty years old, he left his carpentry shop and went south to Judea to join a religious revival movement led by a fiery prophet named John the Baptist. John was announcing that the time was near when God would establish his kingdom on earth. People needed to prepare themselves, so they should turn from their sins, return to God, and be baptized.

Jesus was one of the many who were baptized by John in the River Jordan, and this seemed to mark a new beginning for him. Sensing the call of God, he returned to Galilee and began to travel around the villages, preaching in the synagogues and healing people, and gathering a group of followers. His message was similar to John's: "The time has come…The kingdom of God has come near. Repent and believe the good news!" (Mark 1.15 NIV). But he went further; he also invited people to believe in *him*, and to follow him.

Word soon got around, and people started wondering: could Jesus be the Messiah, the king God had promised, the one who would drive out the nation's enemies and set up a new Israel based on justice and holiness? Had the time finally come when God was going to set the world to rights, and was Jesus the one who God would use to do it?

People flocked to see Jesus, mainly because of the remarkable healings and miracles he performed. But his teaching was also attractive. He told them that God was their Father, and every human being was important to God. But God was also the true ruler of the world; other kings and lords might seem to have the upper hand for a while, but their rule wouldn't last.

Wherever Jesus went, crowds gathered, and strange things happened. He healed the sick and set free those who were troubled by evil spirits. At least twice in his ministry, he brought a dead person back to life. All four of the gospels agree about these amazing events.

What kind of person was he? He lived among the poor quite happily, but he also had friends among the rich. He saw the big picture and could be impatient with little details, and this comes out in his teaching: the most important commands, he said, were to love God with all your heart and to love your neighbour as yourself. This was much more important than religious rituals and traditions. Jesus enjoyed parties and good conversations but was often criticized by the religious for keeping bad company. They called him 'friend of sinners,' and they didn't mean it as a compliment.

Thousands of people heard Jesus' teaching, and most of those who believed in him probably went home and tried to practice his new way of life in the context of their own communities. But he also gathered a group of followers and spent a lot of time in intensive teaching with them. Much of the first three gospels is made up of the things he told them, things they most likely memorized and treasured as the years went by. We call those followers his 'disciples', but the word 'apprentice' might be a good modern equivalent.

It's worth noting that it was customary in those days for disciples to choose their own teacher, but Jesus did it the other way around: he called people to follow him. And the people he chose would have raised a few eyebrows; not respectable members of the religious establishment, but fishermen and tax collectors. It's also worth noting that there were twelve of them, the same number as the twelve tribes of Israel. People would have noticed this, and some would perhaps have shaken their heads. What did Jesus think he was doing? Did he think he was a new Moses, gathering a new nation of Israel around him?

Increasingly, the religious establishment opposed Jesus. He was acting as if the Temple in Jerusalem was irrelevant; people could come to him and receive forgiveness without needing to offer a sacrifice. He taught on his own authority, without waiting for proper authorization from the religious leaders. The powerful saw him as a threat, and as time went by, they plotted to get rid of him.

Their plans came to fruition during Jesus' final visit to Jerusalem for the Passover festival, in the third year of his ministry. It was a visit full of symbolism, beginning with a triumphal entry into the city on the back of a donkey, just like the king foretold by one of the old prophets (see Zechariah 9.9-10). This is the only time in his life Jesus is ever recorded as riding a donkey or a horse, and it was clearly intentional. He spent the next few days teaching in the courts of the Temple, taking charge as if he owned the place. Later, on the Thursday evening, he ate a special meal with his disciples, during which he shared bread and wine with them, claiming that these elements were his body and blood, broken and poured out for the forgiveness of sins. He told them to keep on sharing this meal in memory of him.

Later that night he was arrested by the Jewish authorities and taken to the house of the high priest for a hearing. He was convicted on the charge of blasphemy: claiming the right to speak and act in ways that were only appropriate for God. The religious leaders then convinced the Roman governor that Jesus was a threat to the state because he claimed to be the king sent by God to set Israel free. The governor sentenced him to die by crucifixion, the punishment Rome often used for political prisoners and rebels against the empire. So in the morning Jesus was stripped, flogged, and forced to carry his cross out to the place of execution. There they crucified him between two criminals. According to all the gospels, his death came surprisingly fast.

And that should have been the end of him. His followers certainly thought it was; they were ready to go back to Galilee and pick up their lives where they had left off when he called them. But on Sunday morning, everything changed. Women from their group went to the tomb early to finish the job of embalming Jesus' body, but when they got there, they found the stone rolled away and the body gone. As the day went by, reports started to come in of people meeting Jesus alive again. That evening he met a group of his followers in the same room where they had shared the last supper four days before, and he continued to meet with groups and individuals at unexpected times and places over the next six weeks. Gradually it became clear to the disciples that Jesus had been right: God had vindicated him by raising him from the dead. Finally, forty days after his resurrection, Jesus commissioned them to go out, spread the good news, and make new followers for him. Then he left them and ascended into heaven.

This is the basic outline of the story the gospels tell us. But what does the story *mean*? And what is the true identity of the central character in the story, Jesus himself?

~

We begin at a level most people can agree on: almost everyone accepts that **Jesus was a great religious teacher.** His teaching focusses on what he saw as the central issues of life, without getting lost in minor details. And it isn't just theory; it's intensely practical, and it's meant to be lived out, not just discussed. "Everyone, then, who hears these words of mine and *acts on them* will like a wise man who built his house on rock" (Matthew 7.24, emphasis mine).

Jesus' characteristic form of teaching is the parable—a short, pithy little story that invites people to look at their lives from a new angle. A runaway son decides to come home, and instead of being rejected, he's welcomed by his father. A pearl collector sells everything he owns, so he can buy the one pearl he's been dreaming about all his life. A farmer plants seeds in his field and then watches as the plants grow in various kinds of soil. Jesus used stories like these to explain his views on the subjects he cared about most: things like the coming of God's kingdom, or the dangers of loving money more than God, or the importance of forgiveness and loving your neighbour.

There's no getting around the fact that the teaching of Jesus is demanding; in fact, for large periods of its history the institutional church has struggled with parts of it. Jesus told his followers not to accumulate treasure on earth, but to sell their possessions and give to the poor. He taught them not to lord it over others, but to serve one another in love. This was the centre of God's will for us: loving God with all our hearts and loving our neighbours as ourselves. And there was no limit to this command to love: it extended not just to friends and people like us, but to outsiders, strangers needing help, and even enemies.

~

So Jesus is a great religious teacher; almost everyone would agree with that. Many would also agree that **Jesus is a good example to follow.** People are attracted by his direct relationship with God and his obvious delight in doing God's will. He loved and cared for all who came to him, regardless of how they were seen by the rich and powerful. He spoke out fearlessly against sin and corruption in high places but was merciful to the poor and those who knew their desperate need of God's help. And in a patriarchal age, his respect for women and his love for children would have set him apart from most of his contemporaries.

Listen to this story about Jesus. He's in the courts of the Temple in Jerusalem; the crowds are gathered around him, and he's teaching them. But then there's an interruption. The religious leaders drag in a woman caught in the act of adultery (just the woman; the man is nowhere in sight). They make her stand in front of everyone, and then they turn to Jesus. "Teacher, this woman was caught in the very act of committing adultery. In the Law, Moses commanded us to stone such women. Now what do you say?"

They think they've got him, of course. If he disagrees publicly with the Law of Moses, he'll definitely lose a lot of followers. But on the other hand, he's made such a big deal out of love and forgiveness, so if he goes along with the letter of the Law, people will accuse him of being inconsistent.

So what does he do? He bends down and begins to write in the dust with his finger. We're not told what he was writing, but it's a detail so vivid that we just know it comes to us from an eyewitness.

The leaders keep on demanding an answer, and eventually Jesus straightens up and fixes them with his eyes. He says, "Let anyone among you who is without sin be the first to throw a stone at her." Then he stoops down again and continues writing in the dust.

I can imagine the silence, the awkward looks, the guilty expressions. And then, one at a time, the oldest first, people begin to slip away. Eventually only Jesus is left, with the woman standing before him. He straightens up and asks her, "Woman, where are they? Has no one condemned you?"

"No one, sir," she replies.

"Neither do I condemn you. Go your way, and from now on do not sin again."

It's not hard to imagine the impact this incident would have had on its first witnesses. "Let the one who is without sin cast the first stone" has come down to us in our language as a proverb, one of many proverbs that come originally from the lips of Jesus. But in this story it's not just words; it's also lived out in actions – wise and courageous actions that saved a woman's life and demonstrated the love and mercy of God for her. That's the kind of thing Jesus is admired for, even today.

~

We've said that Jesus was *a great religious teacher* and *a good example to follow*. Some would add a third thing about him: he was **a person sent by God.** Many would place Jesus on the list of men and women throughout history who have been given a message from God to deliver to the world. Sometimes we refer to these people as prophets. Nowadays we tend to think of prophets as people who predict the future, but in the Bible, that's not the main thing they do. Prophets are called to speak to people on God's behalf. Often their message is a word of warning: "The direction you're taking is leading to disaster. You're moving further and further from God's good plan for you. Come back to God and live by his teachings."

The Hebrew scriptures include the words of many prophets: Elijah, Isaiah, Jeremiah, Amos. The New Testament adds John the Baptist to their number. Many would put Jesus on that list; some would even give him the first place.

~

But even when we have said all this, there's still a lot more. Several times in the gospels, Jesus announced to individuals that their sins were forgiven. His enemies pointed out that he had no right to say this; only God can forgive sins. And of course, they were correct. If you were to do me an injury, I could certainly choose to forgive you, but if I were to say to you, "My friend, *all your sins* are forgiven," you'd think I was being very presumptuous.

There's more. Jesus tells people that if they obey his teaching they will not die. He claims to be the Way, the Truth, and the Life; if you come to God, you come through him. He says, "Whoever has seen me has seen the Father." After his resurrection, when his follower Thomas kneels in front of him and cries out "My Lord and my God!" Jesus doesn't say, "No, Thomas, you have it all wrong. I'm not God; I'm just an ordinary preacher." He says, "Have you believed because you have seen me? Blessed are those who have not seen and yet have come to believe" (See John 8.51-53, John 14.6-9, and John 20:29).

So here we have a man who seems very close to God. His teaching is universally admired. He has unusual powers to heal the sick, cares for the poor and the outcast, devotes himself to doing God's will, and calls others to do the same. And yet, he seems to make such outrageous claims for himself!

What would we have said about this man? One thing we probably *wouldn't* have said is "He's a great religious teacher!" If I said the sort of thing Jesus said, I doubt if my congregation would conclude, "Tim's a great preacher, but he's a bit confused about his own divinity!" No: they'd probably dismiss me on the spot!

So on the one hand, we have the simple goodness of Jesus' character, the obvious wisdom of his teaching and the power of his example. On the other hand, we have the extraordinary claims he seems to make for himself. How do we reconcile these things? Well, let me introduce you to the Gospel according to Calvin and Hobbes.

Calvin and Hobbes are characters created by Bill Watterson in his comic strip of the same name. This precocious six-year-old boy and his stuffed tiger are very important figures in our family.

Imagine this: one day, Calvin and Hobbes have an argument about the existence of the Great Cartoonist. How did their comic strip come about? Is there a Great Cartoonist out there, who lives in a much bigger world? Is he the one who created them and controls everything they say and do? Or is he a myth?

Calvin says, "*Of course* there's a Great Cartoonist! His name's Bill Watterson, he created everything in this comic strip, and he's controlling all our actions!" Hobbes replies, "But how do we *know* that? There's no evidence that he even exists! As far as we know, this comic strip is the whole universe. There's nothing else."

As Bill Watterson watches this debate, he gets more and more frustrated. He wants his characters to know he exists, but he can't reach them. Finally he comes up with a plan. He draws *himself* as a character in the comic strip, walking up to Calvin and Hobbes. "Hi guys!" he says. "I'm Bill and I'm the Great Cartoonist! I dreamed you up from my fertile imagination!"

How would they respond? I imagine Calvin bowing down in awe. "O Great Cartoonist! I always knew you were there! I'm sorry for all the things I did to Mom and Dad and Suzy and Mo, and could you please do something about the monsters under my bed?"

But what does Hobbes say? I imagine him stroking his tiger whiskers with a sceptical expression on his face. "How do we know you're the so-called 'Great Cartoonist'? You don't look any different from us. How do we know you aren't just another character in the comic strip?"

And think of God, the Creator of all, trying to communicate with us, so that we can believe that he exists, that he loves us more than we can imagine, and that he wants to rescue us from evil and sin and lead us into freedom and new life. Imagine God finally deciding that the only way to get this message through to us is to come and live among us as one of us, to live and die and rise again to save us.

That's the story the gospels are telling us. That's what was happening in Bethlehem and Nazareth, in Bethsaida and Cana, in Bethany and Jerusalem. That's who Jesus is. Yes, he's a great religious teacher, a good example for us to follow, a man sent by God, a true prophet. But he's more than that. In some way beyond our human comprehension, God was able to continue to live as God of the whole universe, while at the same time writing himself into the story of our planet as one of us. The author of the Gospel of John expressed it like this:

> In the beginning was the Word, and the Word was with God, and the Word was God...And the Word became flesh and lived among us, and we have seen his glory, the glory as of a father's only son, full of grace and truth. (John 1.1, 14)

~

Jesus' death

If we're right about who Jesus is, then it's a truly astounding thing that he should *die*. Most people who believe in gods take it for granted that those gods are immortal. How is it possible that God should share our death?

Even more astounding is the idea that God would allow himself to be executed by those who hated him. Surely God is more powerful than any human being, any country, any organization, any villain or tyrant or murderer! Why on earth would God allow himself to be defeated?

We can begin to answer this question when we grasp the depth of God's determination to share our human life. One of the writers of the New Testament put it like this:

> This High Priest of ours (i.e. Jesus) understands our weaknesses, for he faced all of the same testing we do, yet he did not sin. So let us come boldly to the throne of our gracious God. There we will receive his mercy, and we will find grace to help us when we need it most. (Hebrews 4.15-16 NLT)

'He faced all the same testing we do'; think about this phrase for a minute. Jesus was born in a borrowed room far from home. When he was about two years old his family had to run away to Egypt to escape from Herod's death squads; he knows what it's like to be a refugee. Later he returned to Nazareth, where he grew up in a country under Roman occupation. He seems to have lost his earthly father, Joseph, at a young age, so he was, as the King James Version put it, 'acquainted with grief' (Isaiah 53.3 KJV).

When he began his active ministry at the age of about thirty, he quickly became a polarizing figure. Powerful and fanatical people opposed him, and some of them thought they were serving God by trying to kill him. He endured hunger and thirst, exhaustion and loneliness, misunderstanding and slander. At one point even the members of his own family accused him of being out of his mind. And then, after three years of active ministry, he was arrested and subjected to an unjust trial, convicted on false charges, and handed over to the Romans to be stripped, flogged, nailed to a cross and left to die. He was buried far from home in a tomb lent by a stranger.

"Can God understand our human struggles?" An English minister asked this question during the First World War, as he was confronted with the spectacle of young men coming home, broken by the horrors of trench warfare. But when he meditated on the sufferings of Jesus, the Rev. Edward Shillito found comfort. Listen to the last verse of his poem 'Jesus of the Scars':

> The other gods were strong; but thou wast weak;
> They rode, but thou didst stumble to a throne;
> But to our wounds only God's wounds can speak,
> And not a god has wounds, but thou alone.

So one way of answering the question of why Jesus died would be to say that it was an integral part of his becoming fully human. He wasn't play-acting; he has truly lived our life and shared our sufferings. God has become one of us.

But the writers of the New Testament go further: they claim that in some way the death of Jesus has 'saved' us. What can that possibly mean?

Obviously, when we're talking about acts of God, we're attempting to describe something far beyond human explanation. As someone once said, "If you think you understand it, it's probably not God!" But when rational explanation falls short, illustrations and metaphors can sometimes come to our aid. Here are three examples of how the early Christians used metaphor to explore the riches of what Jesus has done for us:

- They described human beings as slaves of evil and sin, and they saw the death of Jesus as the price paid to set us free (the word used in the New Testament is 'redeem' or 'ransom').
- They saw Jesus as our leader in the decisive battle against the forces of evil. At the crucial point in the battle, he went forward courageously and gave his life for us. As a result of his death, the great victory over the power of evil has been won forever.
- They saw humans as rebels against God who have already begun to suffer the consequences of their rebellion. But Jesus

shows us how much God loves us by taking our suffering on his own shoulders, so we can go free.

These are just three of the metaphors used in the New Testament to try to understand the death of Jesus; there are many others.

But I want to go in a slightly different direction. Listen to these words of Jesus:

> 'You have heard that it was said, "You shall love your neighbour and hate your enemy." But I say to you: Love your enemies and pray for those who persecute you, so that you may be children of your Father in heaven; for he makes his sun rise on the evil and on the good and sends rain on the righteous and on the unrighteous. For if you love those who love you, what reward do you have? Do not even the tax-collectors do the same? And if you greet only your brothers and sisters, what more are you doing than others? Do not even the gentiles do the same? Be perfect, therefore, as your heavenly Father is perfect.' (Matthew 5.43-48)

'Perfect' in this context doesn't mean 'flawless'; it means 'all-encompassing'. When describing God's love, it means no one gets left out—friends or enemies, evil or good. God reaches out to all and showers them with love. This is what Jesus is doing on the Cross: he's imitating the love of his heavenly Father for the righteous and the unrighteous.

Think about this for a moment: How can reconciliation ever take place if both parties refuse to give up their right to hit back? It's impossible. In order for two people to be reconciled, one of them has to be the first to accept the injury and refuse to retaliate.

Now apply this to the story of Jesus' life and death. God comes among us and lives as one of us, and through Jesus, God pours out love and blessing on all who need it. But what do we humans do? We reject God's love and we come together, under our best and strongest leaders, to get rid of the one who embodies it. We do this in the cruelest possible way, by nailing Jesus to a cross and leaving him to die.

In the ancient world, any god worth their salt would have known how to respond to an outrage like that: the perpetrators would have been wiped out in a fit of divine anger. But that's not what Jesus did. Instead of vengeance, he offered forgiveness. "Father, forgive them, for they do not know what they are doing" (Luke 23.34).

This is what the death of Jesus does: it embodies the unconditional love and forgiveness of God. The writers of the New Testament never got over their wonder at this. Listen to Peter and Paul:

> When (Jesus) was insulted, he did not answer back with an insult; when he suffered, he did not threaten, but placed his hopes in God, the righteous Judge. Christ himself carried our sins in his body to the cross, so that we might die to sin and live for righteousness. It is by his wounds that you have been healed. (1 Peter 2.23-24 GNT)

> Our message is that God was making all human beings his friends through Christ. God did not keep an account of their sins, and he has given us the message which tells how he makes them his friends. (2 Corinthians 5.19 GNT)

~

Jesus' resurrection

From earliest times Christians have believed that the Cross wasn't the end for Jesus; rather, as the Apostles' Creed puts it, 'On the third day he rose again from the dead.' What's the evidence for this belief? Consider three things:

~

The empty tomb

After Jesus' death, kind friends placed his body in a private tomb, a small cave in a garden near the place of crucifixion. Because the Jewish leaders were anxious about the disciples stealing the body and claiming that Jesus had been raised from the dead, they asked the Romans to seal the tomb and place a guard on it. The Romans agreed to this, and a squad of four soldiers would have been on duty at the tomb from late Friday evening through to Sunday morning.

The early Christians claimed that a group of women, all devoted followers of Jesus, went to the tomb early on Sunday morning. When they got there, they found that the stone that had been covering the entrance had been rolled away, and the body of Jesus was gone.

Interestingly, none of the opponents of Christianity ever disputed this central fact. How do we know that? Because seven weeks later, when Jesus' followers went out onto the streets of Jerusalem and began to preach that Jesus had been raised from the dead, it would have been the easiest thing in the world for a member of the Jewish Council to have said, "Excuse me; anyone want to take a little trip to his tomb? We can show you the very place, and if you like we can open it up and show you that the body is still there."

If they'd done that, they would have crushed the Christian movement. In fact, it would have been the obvious thing for them to do—*if* the body had still been in the tomb. It was because the body was *not* there that they had to try a different approach.

Down through the centuries, several explanations have been offered for the disappearance of the body of Jesus. One set of possible answers asserts that someone stole the body. Could it have been the work of grave robbers? Perhaps, but if so, how did they get past the Roman guards? And even if they were successful in getting through and opening the tomb, why would they take the body and leave the grave clothes? Grave robbers were interested in the clothes and other treasures left in tombs, not the bodies themselves.

Did Jesus' followers take the body? There are serious problems with this suggestion. First, the disciples were in no state of mind on Good Friday to come up with a plan like that. They were in hiding behind locked doors, afraid that they were about to be arrested. They seem to have forgotten everything Jesus said about his resurrection. As far as they were concerned, the movement was over, they'd been wrong about Jesus, he wasn't the Messiah, and the sooner they got back to Galilee, the safer they would feel. Also, we need to remember the future destiny of these people; in later years many of them were persecuted and killed for what they believed and preached. People aren't usually willing to die for something they know to be a lie.

If the body wasn't stolen by grave robbers or the disciples, did the Jewish leaders or the Roman authorities perhaps take it? If so, why didn't they produce the body when Jesus' followers started to preach that he was risen?

The most ingenious suggestion offered to explain the empty tomb is this: perhaps Jesus wasn't really dead. Perhaps he merely fainted on the Cross, revived in the cool of the tomb, rolled away the stone and staged his own resurrection!

Personally, I think this theory requires more faith than the resurrection. We're asked to believe that Jesus recovered so quickly and completely from his catastrophic injuries that he could single-handedly roll away a stone weighing half a ton. After that, he overpowered four Roman guards, staggered to the place where the disciples were hiding, and convinced them that he wasn't a mortally wounded man in need of medical attention, but their Lord, gloriously raised from the dead!

These are the main alternative explanations that have been offered for the fact that the women found the tomb empty on that Sunday morning. In my view, none of them are persuasive.

~

The testimony of the eyewitnesses

There seem to be minor contradictions in the stories of the eyewitnesses, and this is exactly what we should expect. After all, they were experiencing an astonishing event for which there was no precedent in the history of the world, and when their stories were written down years later, it was inevitable that their memories wouldn't be perfect. Still, when we compare their stories, we can easily discern an essential narrative on which they all agree.

Jesus was buried on Friday afternoon, in a burial cave situated in a garden belonging to one of his admirers, with a stone rolled across its mouth. At sundown on Friday evening the Jewish

Passover began, all the stores closed, and the women weren't able to buy all the spices they needed to do a proper job of preparing Jesus' body for burial. So early on Sunday morning they went back to the tomb to finish the job. When they got there, they found the stone rolled away and the tomb empty. At least one of them, Mary Magdalene, went and told the apostles what had happened. Peter and John went back to the tomb and confirmed her testimony for themselves: it was empty.

Mary had followed them back to the garden, and she stayed there after they returned to the room where the remaining disciples were hiding. She was the first one to actually see Jesus alive. In her excitement she went and told the men, but they dismissed her story as an idle tale.

However, as the day went on, they had cause to reconsider. That same afternoon two followers of Jesus were walking out to a village called Emmaus, seven miles from Jerusalem, when a stranger came and walked alongside them. He listened to their sad story about the events of Good Friday, and then explained to them what the Hebrew scriptures said about the death of the Messiah. When they got to their destination, they invited him in to share a meal with them. During supper, he took bread, gave thanks, broke it, and gave it to them. At that moment it was as if their eyes were fully opened for the first time; they realised it was Jesus, and he immediately vanished from their sight. But there was no doubt in their minds; they ran back to Jerusalem and were in the middle of telling the others about it when Jesus himself appeared in the room. They were afraid, thinking it was a ghost, but when he invited them to touch him, and ate a piece of fish in front of them, they were convinced.

These encounters went on for the next six weeks. Sometimes Jesus appeared to just one person, sometimes to groups, at one time to five hundred people at once. Some of the appearances were in Jerusalem, some in Galilee. Sometimes Jesus was recognized instantly, sometimes there seemed to be something mysterious about his appearance and people didn't recognise him right away.

What are we to make of all these eyewitness stories? Were these people all hallucinating? Hallucinations usually happen to individual people, but Jesus' resurrection appearances were witnessed by both individuals and groups. They don't read at all like hallucinations.

Also, when we consider the role of Mary and the other women, one thing stands out to people familiar with first century Jewish history. In that time and place, women weren't considered to be reliable witnesses. Their testimony wasn't admissible in court. So if you were one of the earliest Christians, and you were making up a fictional story of the resurrection of Jesus, one detail you definitely wouldn't include would be that the first witnesses had been women. In fact, when Paul tells the story of the resurrection, the women are conspicuous by their absence from his witness list (see 1 Corinthians 15.1-11).

But the writers of the gospels refused to take this easy way out. The story as they remembered it included Mary and the other women, and that was how they wrote it down. This is strong evidence of their desire to tell the story as it had actually happened.

~

The change in the disciples

On the night Jesus was arrested, all his disciples ran away in fear and abandoned him. After Jesus' death the next day, they went into hiding behind locked doors. They had no thoughts of continuing the mission Jesus started. In fact, if nothing else had happened after Good Friday, we can be quite sure that the Christian Church wouldn't have taken off the way it did. The apostles might have formed a little 'Jesus Memorial Society' to treasure the memory of the master they had loved, but that would have been as far as it went.

The story the Bible tells us is very different. Six weeks after the death of Jesus, these same apostles marched out onto the streets of Jerusalem and announced boldly, for all the world to hear, that Jesus had been raised from the dead. Peter preached such a powerful sermon that three thousand people became followers of Jesus on the spot. And in the weeks, months, and years ahead, the disciple group clung stubbornly to their belief that Jesus was alive, refusing to give it up even when the Jewish authorities started killing them off. What explains this dramatic change in the disciples? Christians believe the reality of Jesus' resurrection is the best explanation.

These are some of the pieces of evidence we need to consider. Down through the centuries millions of Christians have examined these stories carefully and prayerfully, and have concluded that the best explanation for them is the one the apostles gave: God had raised Jesus from the dead.

~

So what?

We began this chapter by asking why we should consider becoming followers of Jesus. I would like to conclude by saying that the Jesus we have been talking about in this chapter is highly relevant to our deepest human needs. What are some of those needs?

We need *forgiveness and healing for the past.* Many of us are deeply aware of how talented we are at messing things up, for ourselves and for others. But we're also aware of the times *we* have been hurt, and maybe those scars continue to shape us and even control us.

We need *guidance and strength for the present.* If we go to the self-help section of our favourite bookstore, we'll discover that the shelves are groaning under the weight of the books that tell us how we should live our lives. And of course, the authors don't all agree with each other! How do we know which is right? Where can we find true wisdom? And if and when we find it, where can we find the resources to put it into practice? After all, many times our main problem isn't that we don't know what to do; we *do* know it, but we don't seem to be able to live by it.

We need *hope for the future.* We're very aware of the major problems the world faces: deeper and deeper divisions, wars and rumours of wars, environmental catastrophes, global pandemics—to name just a few. Many of us probably also recognize that things aren't looking good in our own lives; we've lost any sense of confidence that the future can be better than the present. And beyond all that, there's the prospect of death; will it be the end, or is there something more to come?

I believe that Jesus provides forgiveness and healing for the past, guidance and strength for the present, and hope for the future.

As we've seen, Jesus' death on the cross is the embodiment of God's forgiving love for all people, even those who reject him. One of the most common phrases on his lips was, "Your sins are forgiven." Forgiveness is at the heart of the Christian message. We're encouraged in many places in the scriptures to come to God, confess our sins and be assured of God's forgiveness.

But what about healing? In my experience as a pastor, some of the most powerful experiences of healing come when we know we're not alone. When people come to me in times of difficulty, often they're not looking for specific answers to problems. What they really want is the comfort of knowing they're not alone, that someone is with them. And many people have begun to find healing from the hurts of the past as they've prayed through them and begun to realize that Jesus was with them. The same Jesus who was rejected and tortured and murdered on the Cross wasn't far away from them in their own experiences of pain.

Jesus provides forgiveness and healing for the past. He also provides guidance and strength for the present. In his teaching he shows us what God's vision for our lives is all about: to grow in love for God, for our neighbour, and for ourselves. He opens up for us the way of forgiveness and generosity, honesty and integrity, love and nonviolence. He identifies the most important things in life—and also the things people *think* are important, but really aren't. And he doesn't only give wise guidance. He also gives strength to put that guidance into practice. In the next chapter we're going to hear about Jesus' promise of the Holy Spirit, who lives in us and gives us the power to follow his teaching and example day by day.

Jesus also provides hope for the future. He teaches us to pray, "Your kingdom come, your will be done, on earth as in heaven." He assures us that the day will come when this prayer is answered—when the new age of compassion and justice and reconciliation will dawn on the world. And he also assures us that death isn't the end for us. As he was raised from the dead, so one day we'll be raised, and we'll live forever in a world fully healed of evil and sin.

Forgiveness and healing for the past; guidance and strength for the present; hope for the future. Surely this is really good news! That's what the old Bible word 'gospel' means: good news. In our next chapter we will think about that good news, and how we can begin to experience it for ourselves.

~

Sources

Allusions to the four gospels occur in numerous places throughout this chapter. It would be good to read at least one of the gospels through in conjunction with this chapter – preferably Mark or Luke.

The short sketch of Jesus' ministry in this chapter owes a lot to Gavin Reid's little book *Our Place in His Story* (Oxford; Bible Reading Fellowship; 1994).

The story of the woman caught in adultery is found in John 7.53 - 8.11.

The line 'Tim's a great preacher; he's just a bit confused about his own divinity' is adapted from Rebecca Manley Pippert: *Out of the Salt Shaker* (Downers Grove; InterVarsity Press; 1979).

I owe the 'Calvin and Hobbes' illustration to Harold Percy; I have heard him use it at several conferences and workshops.

I first came across the poem 'Jesus of the Scars', by Edward Shillito, in John Stott's book *The Cross of Christ*. It is freely available on the internet and to the best of my knowledge is in the public domain. The whole poem is well worth reading and pondering.

My reconstruction of the resurrection appearances of Jesus relies not just on the Gospels but also on Paul's account in 1 Corinthians 15:1-11.

CHAPTER 3:

WHERE DO I FIT IN?

In our last chapter we thought about the person of Jesus. We saw that he's not just a great religious teacher, a good example to follow, or even a remarkable prophet. In him, God has visited this planet. By his life and teaching he shows us what God is like. His death on the Cross is the ultimate embodiment of God's forgiving love for all humanity. And Christians believe the story is still going on, because he was raised from the dead and is alive forever.

But for many of us, this raises the question of how this can be real in our own experience. If Jesus is alive, how can I connect with him? Or is such a thing even possible?

~

What is the Good News?

I sometimes ask people, "If you could sum up the Christian message in one or two sentences, how would you do it?" Nine times out of ten, the answers people give are about *our* behaviour. "Do to others as you would have them do to you." "Love thy neighbour." "Believe in God."

These are all good things, but they're good advice, not good news. Here's the problem: when the early followers of Jesus began spreading his message, they didn't call it 'the good advice.' They called it 'the gospel,' a word that means 'good news.' So whatever else we might want to say about doing to others as we would have them do to us, or loving our neighbour, they can't be the heart of the Christian message; we must find that somewhere else.

I believe there are two aspects of the gospel, or good news, and they complement each other perfectly.

~

The Good News is about the Kingdom of God

Imagine a group of aliens from another planet landing in occupied France in 1942. They'd probably find it to be a country of baffling contrasts. On the one hand, they'd find a beautiful people with an ancient culture, impressive architecture, a long history, magnificent countryside, and many other wonderful things to admire. On the other hand, they'd see people starving, being arrested, and being sent off on trains, never to return. The whole nation would be in a dark and fearful mood. Our aliens would probably be puzzled by the contrast they saw between the beauty and the horror, the light and the darkness.

Now imagine our aliens asking one of the local inhabitants, "What's this all about?" Perhaps one of the locals would reply: "You must understand—this isn't normal for us. There's a war going on, and enemy soldiers have occupied our country. But we're all hoping and longing for the day when we'll be set free; come and see us again then, and you'll have the time of your life!"

During World War Two C.S. Lewis used a striking illustration in a radio talk he gave for the BBC: the world, he said, is 'enemy-occupied territory.' He went on to say that Christianity is the story of how the rightful king has landed in disguise and has begun a great campaign of resistance. We're all invited to be part of that campaign, and we find hope in God's promise that one day, the enemy's stranglehold on our country will be broken, and we'll finally be free.

We can imagine how powerful this illustration would have been to the people who first heard it. At the time, much of Europe was suffering under Nazi tyranny; minorities were being viciously persecuted, beautiful cultures were being plundered, and many lives were destroyed. This would have been a powerful example of how the forces of evil have invaded God's good world and perverted God's good plan.

'The rightful king' in Lewis' illustration is Jesus. As we saw in the last chapter, he began his ministry in Galilee with a dramatic announcement: "The time is fulfilled, and the kingdom of God has come near; repent, and believe in the good news" (Mark 1.15). What did Jesus mean by that?

Perhaps he might have spelled it out like this: "For thousands of years the world has been deceived by the power of evil, and marred by selfishness, anger, hatred, and greed. But now there's good news to share: God isn't going to allow this state of affairs to continue forever. God is at work in the world right now, breaking the power of evil and restoring the world to its original purpose. And one day, evil will be totally wiped out, and God's dream for creation will finally come true. God wants each of you to be part of that. So turn from evil, believe this good news, and follow me."

And there's more. The early Christians believed that Jesus' death and resurrection were actually the decisive victory in God's campaign to liberate the world from evil. Through his death, Jesus has opened the way back to God for all people. In his resurrection, the power of death itself has begun to be reversed. So even though there's still plenty of evil left in the world, Christians believe it's only a matter of time before God eradicates it forever.

In a nutshell, that's what Jesus meant by the phrase 'the kingdom of God,' or 'the reign of God.' The Good News tells us that the kingdom of God is coming—it's already at work in the world—and that's something to celebrate.

~

The Good News is about reconciliation with God.

In our culture today we know a lot about broken relationships, and that makes reconciliation an extremely valuable skill. If you're the kind of person who can help an estranged couple repair their relationship, you're worth big money in our culture. If you know how to help union and management come to an agreement both sides can accept, you'll never be short of work.

According to the Gospel, God is all about reconciliation. The Bible assumes that from the beginning, we humans have quarrelled with our Creator. God gave people guidelines about how to live a full and happy life, in love and holiness. But the first humans were deceived by the power of evil. They came to believe that the way to fulfilment was to reject God's way, and to put themselves at the centre of their own lives. So humanity chose to rebel against God's loving will, and to this day we continue to do so.

What are the consequences of our broken relationship with God? A great Christian writer named Augustine once prayed, 'God, you have made us for yourself, and our hearts are restless until they find rest in you.' Augustine knew we weren't created to live in isolation from God. In fact, our deepest needs can only be met in the context of a living relationship with God. This is sometimes described as having a 'God-shaped hole' in our hearts. We can try to stuff that hole with other things to take away the ache of emptiness (money and possessions are among the most common God-substitutes we use), but in the end, nothing else can take God's place. God-substitutes can't deliver on their promises.

Human beings have realised this for a long time, and the human race has a long history of trying to rebuild its relationship with God. The problem is, we've often tried to accomplish this through our own efforts, rather than through trusting God's love for us. I want to share with you one particular blind alley the human race has often tried; we might call it the way of law.

The way of law is very logical. It starts with a correct assumption: the reason we human beings are estranged from God is because of our disobedience and rebellion. That being the case, it seems logical that the way to repair our relationship with God would be through obedience, so Step 1 in the way of law is to obey God's laws. Everything else depends on this step, and when a person has been successful in this, they can proceed to step 2, which is that God accepts them on the basis of their obedience. Step 3 follows: God gives them loving care by providing for their needs and answering their prayers. And Step 4 is that they know they have a status with God; they are God's servants.

The way of law is fine in theory, but in practice it fails at Step 1. Members of Alcoholics Anonymous have known for a long time that they aren't strong enough in themselves to be free from their addiction to alcohol. The same is true of our addiction to sin. Getting free of it by our own strength—in other words, obeying God's laws as a way of rebuilding our relationship with God—is something we just can't do.

In fact, the way of law tends to produce two different kinds of people, and you will see them very clearly in a story Jesus told in Luke's Gospel.

> Then Jesus told this story to some who had great confidence in their own righteousness and scorned everyone else: "Two men went to the Temple to pray. One was a Pharisee, and the other was a despised tax collector. The Pharisee stood by himself and prayed this prayer: 'I thank you, God, that I am not like other people—cheaters, sinners, adulterers. I'm certainly not like that tax collector! I fast twice a week, and I give you a tenth of my income.'
>
> "But the tax collector stood at a distance and dared not even lift his eyes to heaven as he prayed. Instead, he beat his chest in sorrow, saying, 'O God, be merciful to me, for I am a sinner.' I tell you, this sinner, not the Pharisee, returned home justified before God. For those who exalt themselves will be humbled, and those who humble themselves will be exalted." (Luke 18.9-14 NLT)

The Pharisee represents those who think they're better than they really are, and the tax collector, those who think they're worse than they really are. The Pharisee believes he's been successful in obeying God's laws, so he has an inside track to the kingdom of God. He also believes he has the right to look down on others who don't measure up to God's standards. He's smug, self-satisfied, self-righteous, and judgmental. We can probably all think of people like the Pharisee; perhaps we've sometimes been like him ourselves.

The tax-collector, on the other hand, thinks he's worse than he really is. He knows he hasn't been successful in following God's laws. He doesn't measure up, and he's under no illusion that he has any right to come close to God. He longs to know God, but his sense of guilt makes him fearful, shy, and wary of anything to do with religion. We can probably think of people like him; maybe we even feel like him ourselves from time to time.

A lot of people think the way of law is Christianity, but in fact it's not. What Jesus gives us is not the way of law, but the way of grace.

It starts with the cross and what Jesus did there. As we read in the last chapter, on the cross Jesus embodies the forgiving love of God for all people, despite the fact that we've rejected that love so many times. Instead of taking vengeance on those who tortured and murdered him, Jesus prayed "Father, forgive them." When one of the criminals crucified with him asked him for mercy, Jesus said, "Truly I tell you, today you will be with me in paradise." (Luke 23.43)

What do we learn from this? We learn that we don't have to wait to make ourselves acceptable before we come; we come as we are, in repentance and faith, and we experience Step 1: God accepts us *unconditionally*.

Having been accepted by God, we then move on to Step 2: we experience God's loving care. God's love comes to us in many ways: through the Holy Spirit who comes to live in us; through the scriptures, which the Holy Spirit inspired to instruct us; through the sacraments which nourish our life in Jesus; through the church, the Christian family supporting and encouraging us. These are just a few of the ways we experience the loving care of God.

Then comes Step 3. In the way of law, our status was that of servants of God, but in the way of grace we're welcomed into God's family as God's sons and daughters. The difference is that if you're dissatisfied with a servant, you can always fire them, but your sons and daughters are in the family for life.

In the way of law, doing God's will was Step 1, but in the way of grace, it's Step 4. Doing God's will is important, but the good news is that it's not the thing our entire relationship with God depends on. Instead, it's the natural consequence of our being loved and accepted. When we fail—as we will—this doesn't jeopardize our life with God. We simply admit it, go back to the unconditional love of Jesus, ask God to forgive us, and ask for help to try again.

This is illustrated beautifully for us in Jesus' story of the prodigal son, which is worth quoting in full:

> To illustrate the point further, Jesus told them this story: "A man had two sons. The younger son told his father, 'I want my share of your estate now before you die.' So his father agreed to divide his wealth between his sons.
>
> "A few days later this younger son packed all his belongings and moved to a distant land, and there he wasted all his money in wild living. About the time his money ran out, a great famine swept over the land, and he began to starve. He persuaded a local farmer to hire him, and the man sent him into his fields to feed the pigs. The young man became so hungry that even the pods he was feeding the pigs looked good to him. But no one gave him anything.
>
> "When he finally came to his senses, he said to himself, 'At home even the hired servants have food enough to spare, and here I am dying of hunger! I will go home to my father and say, "Father, I have sinned against both heaven and you, and I am no longer worthy of being called your son. Please take me on as a hired servant."'
>
> "So he returned home to his father. And while he was still a long way off, his father saw him coming. Filled with love and compassion, he ran to his son, embraced him, and kissed him. His son said to him, 'Father, I have sinned against both heaven and you, and I am no longer worthy of being called your son.'
>
> "But his father said to the servants, 'Quick! Bring the finest robe in the house and put it on him. Get a ring for his finger and sandals for his feet. And kill the calf we have been fattening. We must celebrate with a feast, for this son of mine was dead and has now returned to life. He was lost, but now he is found.' So the party began.

> "Meanwhile, the older son was in the fields working. When he returned home, he heard music and dancing in the house, and he asked one of the servants what was going on. 'Your brother is back,' he was told, 'and your father has killed the fattened calf. We are celebrating because of his safe return.'
>
> "The older brother was angry and wouldn't go in. His father came out and begged him, but he replied, 'All these years I've slaved for you and never once refused to do a single thing you told me to. And in all that time you never gave me even one young goat for a feast with my friends. Yet when this son of yours comes back after squandering your money on prostitutes, you celebrate by killing the fattened calf!'
>
> "His father said to him, 'Look, dear son, you have always stayed by me, and everything I have is yours. We had to celebrate this happy day. For your brother was dead and has come back to life! He was lost, but now he is found!'" (Luke 15.11-32 NLT)

As the younger son trudged the weary miles back to his father's house, his thoughts were very much along the lines of the way of law: "I am no longer worthy of being called your son. Please take me on as a hired servant."

But what did the father do? He felt compassion for his son; he ran to him, hugged him and kissed him, restored him to his position in the family, and threw a party to celebrate his return. This wasn't the sort of reception the younger son had been expecting. His broken relationship with his father was mended through the father's unconditional love. This is what God has done for us in Jesus. When we come home, God welcomes us back into the family.

God is passionate about reconciliation. I love the way one of the early Christian writers, Paul, sums this up:

> 'Anyone who is joined to Christ is a new being; the old is gone, the new has come. All this is done by God, who through Christ changed us from enemies into his friends

> and gave us the task of making others his friends also. Our message is that God was making all human beings his friends through Christ.' (2 Corinthians 5.17-19a GNT)

You might say that the whole gospel story is the story of God coming to the human race and saying, 'Can we be friends?' We're invited to come home to God like the prodigal son, put our faith in Jesus, and experience the heavenly Father's welcome. That's the Good News of reconciliation with God.

~

How Do I Respond to the Good News?

If you ask followers of Jesus from different churches how you become a Christian, you'll sometimes get very different replies. One person might tell you, "You become a Christian by being baptized." Another might say "No—you need to ask Jesus to come into your heart as your personal Lord and Saviour." A third might say, "You have to have an experience of the Holy Spirit." But I say, why choose among them? In the New Testament, all three are important.

~

Baptism

People sometimes say, "Baptism doesn't do anything for you; it's just a symbol." But to say that something is *just* a symbol is to fail to understand the tremendous power of symbols. Years ago my wife Marci made a trip to Ontario to visit her relatives. I drove her to the airport, but when we got there, she realized she'd accidentally left her wedding ring behind. I drove back to our house, found the ring, and brought it to her before the plane left. Neither of us thought of saying, "It's just a symbol." It meant a great deal to both of us that she should have her wedding ring with her on the trip, as a symbol of our marriage.

In New Testament times Christianity was very much a minority religion and the decision to be baptized was usually made by adults who were aware of the possible unpleasant consequences. This is still true in some parts of the world. A friend of mine who spent some time as a missionary in Japan once told me that when Japanese young people made the decision to become Christians publicly, by being baptized, that was the moment at which strict Buddhist parents sometimes disowned them. They understood what the action of baptism meant.

In the New Testament there are lots of ways of describing what baptism does for us. Sometimes it's compared to a bath; the dirt of our sins is washed away, and we stand clean before God. Sometimes going down into the water is seen as dying with Jesus, and coming up out of the water is seen as rising to new life with him. Sometimes it's seen as a sign of a new birth into God's family.

I think in our modern world, it makes sense to many people to see baptism as the beginning of a life of following Jesus; we could even describe it as *enrolment in the school of Jesus.* Listen to what Jesus said to his first followers:

> "Go therefore and make disciples of all nations, baptizing them in the name of the Father and of the Son and of the Holy Spirit, and teaching them to obey everything I have commanded you" (Matthew 28:18-20a).

Baptism isn't a way of giving a baby a name or protecting the baby from the horrible things that might happen to it if it were to die unbaptized. Rather, whether you're baptized as a child or as an adult, your baptism is the beginning of a life of following Jesus.

~

The Gift of the Holy Spirit

A second part of becoming a Christian in the New Testament is something I find absolutely amazing. The Holy Spirit, who is God at work in the world, comes to live in each person who becomes a Christian.

In ancient times most ships were equipped with two methods of propulsion: oars (usually worked by slaves) and sails. Oars were useful when there was no wind, or when the wind was blowing in the wrong direction. But if the wind was blowing in the right direction, only a very foolish captain would continue to use rowers; the wind in the sails was a far more efficient source of energy.

In the original languages of the Bible, the word for wind is the same as the word for spirit. The gift of the Holy Spirit means that Christians aren't completely dependent on their own resources, like slaves rowing a ship. Instead, the Spirit who lives in us is a whole new source of energy for us as we try to do the things Jesus taught us. And this makes all the difference.

Sometimes people have very deep experiences of the power of the Holy Spirit. Our society can be quite sceptical about this sort of thing, so people often keep their stories to themselves, and most people are unaware of how widespread these experiences are.

Let me tell you about the experience of someone I knew quite well: my dad. He had been praying for a number of years for a deeper experience of the Holy Spirit. Here's how he described what happened to him:

> On Shrove Tuesday 1971, I was part of an ecumenical prayer group, and all the members knew that I was waiting, in obedience to the Lord, to be filled with the Holy Spirit. Two of the group asked me if I would like them to pray with me. I agreed and they prayed, but nothing happened. I was trying to will myself into the experience, but that isn't how it happens. So in my heart I prayed, "Well, Lord, I've waited twelve years, I can wait longer, if that's what you want." And that was what the Lord was waiting for...And so it happened. My heart was bursting with a joy and peace and love I had never known before.
>
> The way I would describe it is that it was like standing under a great waterfall. The water not only cleansed the outside, but poured through the whole body, soaking and enriching every cell. I realized that every drop of that water was the Spirit's power filling me to overflowing with the love of Jesus.

Not everyone has a dramatic experience like this, and if you've never had one, that doesn't mean you're a second-class Christian.

However, many Christians would testify that deeper experiences of the Holy Spirit are far more accessible than we realise. And perhaps even more important than a dramatic experience is the way the Holy Spirit quietly gives people strength to follow the Christian way.

A friend of mine who had recently become a Christian went through a very stressful experience, which he expected to make him angry and belligerent. To his surprise, he found he was responding in a much more peaceful way. This puzzled him, and he was still thinking about it the following Sunday when he went to church. The truth hit him as he went forward to receive Holy Communion. "As I held out my hands to receive the bread," he said, "it came to me that I had help—help I hadn't had before."

That was the work of the Holy Spirit. God gives the Holy Spirit to all followers of Jesus, and God invites us to grow daily in our experience of the Spirit's power.

~

Faith

The third part of becoming a Christian is described in the Bible as 'faith'—or, as we might say more commonly today, 'trust'. To 'believe in Jesus' is not just to believe Jesus exists, but to *trust* Jesus—to trust him with your life. When you go to a doctor, you're putting your life in her hands. If she's a good doctor, it's easy for you to trust her and follow her instructions without hesitation, knowing that if you do so, you'll get well. This is the kind of faith Jesus inspires in us.

On 1 March 1979 I asked Marci to marry me. We'd been talking and praying about it for some time, and I wasn't seriously expecting a refusal, but I must admit there were butterflies in my stomach that morning when I went over to her place to propose to her. 'Yes' is such a tiny word, but in certain contexts it can change your life irrevocably.

Christians believe that in the Good News, God is giving us an invitation that can change our lives. Jesus is inviting each of us to turn away from God-substitutes, put our trust in him, and follow him as his disciples with the help of the Holy Spirit.

If you're like me, before you make a decision about an offer like this you want to read the fine print. Perhaps you're thinking "So Jesus wants me to follow him, does he? Well, I'm prepared to consider that, but first I want to know where he's going to lead me." Fortunately for us, the scriptures aren't backward in giving us an answer to this question. When we say yes to Jesus' invitation to follow him, we're saying yes to three things.

First, we're saying yes to **a new relationship with God.** Jesus wants to show us how to live our lives with God at the centre, and everything else finding its proper place around God. So we'll be getting to know God better and learning to love, trust and obey God. Two of the ways we learn to do that are by listening for God's voice and speaking to God, as we read the Bible and pray.

Second, we're saying yes to **the people of God.** Jesus never called people to follow him by themselves; he always called them to be part of a community. In the same way today, when we follow Jesus we do so in the company of other Christians. So being a disciple of Jesus means participating in his church and learning to love and be loved by our fellow disciples.

Thirdly, we're saying yes to **the values of God's kingdom.** God's kingdom is sometimes described as an upside-down kingdom, because its values are completely different from the world's values. So we can expect some conflict, both with our neighbours and with our own inner selfishness, as we try to learn the new way of life Jesus is teaching us.

I'll spell out these three things in more detail later on in this book, but for now I want to return to the idea of responding to God. People tend to be at different stages in terms of that response of faith. Let's look at the 'response grid' in our diagram below:

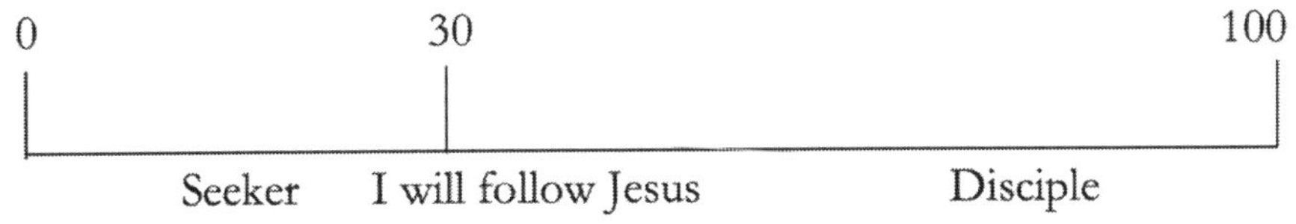

For the sake of this illustration, a person at the extreme left of the grid is in the very beginning stages of their journey with Christ. A person at the extreme right, on the other hand, is a seasoned disciple of Jesus with a much fuller knowledge of Christian truth and a much greater experience of putting it into practice.

'30' is the point at which a person comes to believe that Jesus is the key to knowing God, and so they wholeheartedly commit their life to Jesus in faith. I call people to the left of 30 'seekers.' Seekers sincerely want to know God, but they aren't convinced about Jesus yet. They have questions like, "What's God like?" "Who is Jesus and why is he important?" and so on.

I call people to the right of 30 'disciples'. Disciples have committed themselves to following Jesus. They have a different set of questions: "How do I read the Bible in a helpful way? How do I pray? How do I put the teaching of Jesus into practice in my personal life, my home and family and professional life? How does my faith impact my leisure time, my volunteering, my giving, and my political convictions?" These are just a few of the questions disciples of Jesus wrestle with.

Let me ask you four questions about this response grid.

First, *where are you on this line?* Perhaps in your mind you'd like to put an 'x' where you think you are today.

Second, *do you want to move further along the line?*

Third, if you do want to move further, *what kind of help do you need?* Are there questions you need answers for, or is there teaching and guidance you need on certain issues? Are there struggles you need to talk through with someone, or commitments you need to make and keep?

Fourth, *will you say yes* at this moment to God's invitation to move further along this line?

It may be that some people reading this book are ready to make that leap from 29 to 31; they want to say, "Yes, now I see that Jesus is the key to knowing God, so I want to put my faith in him today and begin to follow him." If that's true for you, I'd invite you to make that response to him. I end this chapter by sharing with you a prayer a lot of people have found helpful in making that response.

> Lord Jesus, I realise that you already know me and that you love me. Now I want to get to know you too. Please forgive me for everything in my life that comes between us, and help me to renounce it as I learn to live the life of God's kingdom. Help me to follow you faithfully, and to grow to love you more and more. Amen.

~

Sources

My outline of the Good News is based on Harold Percy's 'Three 'R's of the Gospel' presentation.

C.S. Lewis' illustration about 'enemy-occupied territory' is found in *Mere Christianity,* Chapter 2. The book is available from several publishers in different editions.

The 'Way of Law'/'Way of Grace' idea is based on a model developed by Frank Lake in *Clinical Theology* (London; Darton, Longman and Todd; 1966). It was passed on to me by the Rev. Lloyd Howard when I was his parish assistant in the late 1970s.

The formulation of saying yes to a new relationship with God, yes to the people of God, and yes to the values of God's kingdom comes from Harold Percy's workshops.

The 'response grid' comes from John Bowen, former director of the Wycliffe College Institute of Evangelism, and was passed on to me by Harold Percy. Harold is also the author of the prayer at the end of the chapter, which comes from his book *Good News People* (Toronto; Anglican Book Centre; 1996), 128.

CHAPTER 4:

WHERE DO I GO FROM HERE?

We ended the last chapter at a point of decision: Will I accept Jesus' invitation to move further along in my relationship with God? Having accepted that Jesus is the key to knowing God, will I commit myself to living with God at the centre of my life, and learning the ways of God's kingdom from Jesus?

If my answer is 'Yes', then what comes next? If I've become a follower of Jesus, where is Jesus leading me?

In Matthew 10.25 Jesus says, "It is enough for the disciple to be like the teacher." In context, Jesus is warning his disciples that if he's been harassed by people opposed to his mission, his followers can expect the same thing. However, the principle also has a wider application. The goal of a disciple isn't just to learn information from the teacher. The goal is *to become like the teacher.* As another New Testament writer says, 'Christ also suffered for you, leaving you an example, so that you should follow in his steps.' (1 Peter 2.21).

Why are we called to become like Jesus? Because Jesus not only shows us what God is like; he also shows us what *we* were designed to be like. I don't mean we're called to dress in first-century clothing, wear sandals, leave our jobs and tramp around the countryside. I mean we're called to internalize the central principles of Jesus: love for God and love for neighbour. In every situation he faced, Jesus chose the way of love. As we follow him, he'll teach us to do the same.

Let's explore how Jesus does that by taking a closer look at the small print. As I mentioned in the last chapter, we are asked to say 'yes' to a new relationship with God, 'yes' to the people of God, and 'yes' to the values of God's kingdom.

~

A New Relationship with God

On the night before he died, Jesus prayed for his disciples:

> "Father, the hour has come; glorify your Son so that the Son may glorify you, since you have given him authority over all people, to give eternal life to all whom you have given him. And this is eternal life, that they may know you, the only true God, and Jesus Christ whom you have sent" (John 17:1-3).

In this prayer Jesus defines eternal life for us: it's not about *how long* we live (living forever in heaven after we die) so much as the *quality of life* we enjoy. The way to enjoy the best quality of life is to know the only true God, and Jesus Christ whom he has sent. Notice that Jesus doesn't say "that they may know *about* you," but "that they may *know* you."

I think the most important disciplines for making this personal knowledge of God a reality in our lives are *prayer* and *reading the Bible*.

A few days after I committed my life to Christ as a thirteen-year-old, my father gave me a little booklet called *Seven Minutes with God*. It was intended to be a help for people who had never prayed or read the Bible seriously before, and it laid out a helpful framework for this. It was very specific about time allocations – half a minute of opening prayer, four minutes of Bible reading, half a minute of adoration and so on. Of course, it assumed that people would soon grow beyond that framework, but the framework was still a good place to start. I was attracted to this idea, and since then I've tried to make prayer and Bible reading a part of my daily routine.

We know how human relationships work; if you seriously care for a person, you make quality time for them. Marci and I find that if we don't go for regular walks together and have times out for coffee when we can give our full attention to each other, our relationship begins to suffer. And if we're going to live in relationship with God, we have to make regular time for that relationship to grow.

Most of us are busy people, and Jesus was no stranger to this. In the first chapter of Mark's Gospel we read about a 'day in the life' of Jesus, including preaching in the synagogue, healing the sick, and casting out demons until late at night. The temptation to sleep late the following morning must have been very strong. But Jesus made a different choice. He knew that just as his body needed rest, his spirit also needed the refreshment of contact with his Father in heaven.

But there was a problem: Jesus was probably staying in a one-room house with no privacy for personal prayer, and he knew that once the household was on the move in the morning the opportunity would be lost. So Mark tells us, 'In the morning, while it was still very dark, he got up and went out to a deserted place, and there he prayed' (Mark 1:35).

I don't think Jesus did this on the spur of the moment. I don't think he woke up, stretched, and thought to himself "Wow! I feel amazingly rested! I think I'll get up and spend some time with God!" Human nature doesn't often work that way. It seems more likely to me that before he went to sleep, Jesus had already decided to get up early so he could go out for a prayer walk. It was a regular part of his daily routine.

So I want to recommend the habit of daily prayer and Bible reading as a very important component of our personal walk with God. If this is new to you, let me suggest a simple framework to start with. This framework has two parts: listening and responding.

First comes **listening**. Remember: the purpose of a time of prayer and Bible reading is to deepen our relationship with God. In that relationship, God is the senior partner, so God gets the first word.

Many people find it helpful to begin a time of prayer with silence, for at least a minute. In that silence we can remind ourselves of who it is we want to meet: the Lord God Almighty, the creator of the universe, but also the one who isn't far away, but is very close to all of us. Some of us might find it helpful during that time of silence to have a visual focus, perhaps a cross on our wall, or a lighted candle on a table beside us. For some people, just the act of lighting their candle helps prepare their minds and hearts to meet with God.

The second part of listening is reading the Bible. If we've never read the Bible seriously before, it would be good to start with one of the first three Gospels—Matthew, Mark, or Luke—and read through it in an orderly way.

Here's a method of reading I recommend. Take a passage, read it through at least twice, and then ask questions like these:

- What is this passage about?
- Is there a promise God wants me to hear and receive?
- Is there a command to obey?
- Is there a warning to heed?
- Is there a good example to follow or a bad one to avoid?
- Do I identify with any of the characters in this story?
- If I were to put the teaching of this passage into practice, what concrete changes would I need to make?

Some people find it helpful to write down the things that come to them in answer to those questions.

The second part of our time with God is **responding**; that's what spoken prayer is all about. Jesus had a very simple way of approaching God. When his disciples asked him to teach them a model prayer, the first word he gave them was *Abba,* which is very close in meaning to the English word *Daddy*. In that spirit of simplicity, I want to suggest to you that we learn the essentials of prayer in kindergarten, and we learn them in four words or phrases.

The first phrase is **thank you**; each day we can say a special thank-you for the blessings God has given us. It's a good idea to be specific about this: name the blessings one by one, and thank God for each of them.

The second word is **sorry**. Every day of our lives we're going to slip up and fall into sin in some way. When we do that we'll hurt God, and in any relationship, when one of the parties hurts the other, the only way forward is sincere apology and forgiveness. The scriptures assure us that God is more than ready to forgive. For our part, we simply have to admit to God what we've done and ask for forgiveness and help so we can learn to do things differently.

The third word is **please**. This is when we bring our concerns to God—for others, and for ourselves. Once again, scripture assures us that God wants to hear our requests, so we don't need to be shy about making them. Many people find it helpful to make a prayer list for themselves, recording not only the names of people they pray for regularly, but also the particular requests they make, perhaps even including the date of the original prayer. It's a great help to faith when we look back over our list and discover that God has granted a request we made not very long ago.

The fourth phrase is **You're awesome!** This phrase isn't actually part of the kindergarten curriculum, but every kid learns it anyway. This part of prayer is sometimes called praise and worship. When we stand next to a natural wonder such as Niagara Falls or Mount Robson, we are often overawed and struggle to find words to express our feelings. Similarly, as a well-known worship song says, 'Our God is an awesome God,' and in praise and worship we try to express our awe.

These four phrases or words sum up almost everything we might want to say to God. We can use them in any order, and we can take as long or as short a time as we need over each word.

How long does this take? If you're a beginner, then probably ten or fifteen minutes a day will help you get into the habit. As you get on in the Christian life you'll probably find that you want to use more time. I've been taking time with God daily since I was thirteen, and I find now that I average about half an hour each morning.

Each of us will also need to find a time and a place that works for us. There are many options. I know people who read the Bible and pray on commuter trains or in their offices before their working day begins. I know parents who pray at home after the children have gone to school, and businesspeople who pray in coffee bars on their lunch break. Others prefer to take their time with God in the quiet of the evening, or at the other end of the day during their morning walk. Some Christians buy the Bible in audio format and listen to it as they commute to work every day.

There are no rules about this. I'm an early morning person and for over forty years I've been making my morning cup of tea or coffee and then turning to my Bible for my time with God before anyone else in the house is awake. That works well for me. I encourage you to find a time that works for you personally, and then make a habit of using it to develop your relationship with God.

~

The Family of God

When Jesus walked the earth for the three years of his public ministry, he didn't write a book, start an institution, or put up a building. What he did was to gather a community of disciples around him. From the very beginning, all Christians were members of this community. There was never an option to follow Jesus alone, because learning to get along with one another and love one another was an integral part of the discipleship process. Not surprisingly, when the followers of Jesus went out all over the world to spread the gospel, they followed their Master's example and started little communities themselves, and so the Christian church was born.

There has never been a time in the history of Christianity when these communities of believers have been perfect. Human gatherings always have tensions and struggles, and churches are no exception. They are communities of flawed and imperfect people, and naturally there are times when those flaws and imperfections show. As a well-known preacher used to say, "If you find the perfect church, don't join it—you'll spoil it!"

The Christian church we read about in the New Testament exists for four purposes: worship, fellowship, learning and mission.

In *worship,* it gathers together week by week to praise God, to listen to the word of God, and to share the meal Jesus left to us.

In *fellowship*, it provides support for individual Christians who would be discouraged and in danger—like sheep straying away from a flock—if they tried to follow Jesus alone.

In *learning*, the Christian community listens to the words of scripture, and its members support one another in putting into practice the new way of life of God's kingdom.

In *mission*, the church reaches out to others with the message of the Good News, and with the love of Jesus shared in practical and caring ways.

I sometimes hear people say, "I don't go to church, but you don't have to go to church to be a Christian." I always feel like replying, "Says who?" There are no examples in the New Testament of Christians who were not part of a church, with the exception of the criminal on the cross who died beside Jesus, and he had a good excuse!

But I do need to clarify a couple of things. First, the main issue is not *going* to church but being *part* of the church. When the Book of Acts records the ongoing conversions of people in Jerusalem, it says "And day by day the Lord added to their number those who were being saved." (Acts 2:47). Notice that these people were experiencing a new relationship with God on an individual level ('being saved'), but they were also becoming members of a specific community of disciples ('their number').

The second point of clarification has to do with how we define church. It's important to remember that in the early years of Christianity the church had no buildings, no professional ministers, no written liturgies, and no printed Bibles. Sunday was an ordinary working day, so gatherings for worship were probably in the early morning or late evening. They were held in people's homes, so they were likely very small, and all indications are that they included a shared meal.

So when I claim that church membership is essential to Christian discipleship, I'm not saying we all need to go to a traditional church, with Sunday morning services held in a building and led by trained clergy. This is one possible form of Christian community—perhaps still the most common form in the western world—but it's not the only form. Around the world today, some Christians meet in huge cathedrals, or mega-churches spread over several locations and linked by video conferencing. Others meet in small home-based gatherings, sometimes with one person watching the door in case the secret police come calling. Other gatherings take place over the Internet (I wrote this chapter during the Covid-19 pandemic, when virtual services became the norm for huge numbers of Christians). All these—and many more besides—are perfectly valid forms of Christian community.

The Christian writer Max Lucado tells of a time when he was speaking at a weekend conference in Boston. Having given his address on the Saturday, he decided to go out to a Boston Celtics basketball game, because they were playing his favourite team, the San Antonio Spurs. As he took his seat for the game, it occurred to him that he might be the only Spurs fan in the crowd, so he might be wise to be quiet. But it was hard! He contained himself for a few moments, but by the end of the first quarter he was letting out solo war-whoops every time the Spurs scored. People were beginning to turn and look.

But then he noticed someone across the aisle who was also applauding for the Spurs. Immediately he felt like he had an ally. They were buoying each other up, and Lucado felt better. At the end of the quarter they gave each other a thumbs-up. The other guy was a teenager, and Lucado was much older, but that didn't matter. They were united by their common support for the Spurs.

In our world, being a Christian can feel lonely at times. There aren't many people who cheer at the same time as us. That's one of the major reasons we need to come together with our fellow Christians. Alone we can easily be intimidated, but together we can be strong.

We saw that there are two disciplines to help us grow in our personal relationship with God: prayer and Bible reading. Similarly, there are two disciplines to help us grow in our relationship with the family of God: corporate worship, and small group fellowship.

From the very beginning, Christians have gathered in **corporate worship**. Jesus gave us one service, the eucharist or Holy Communion, and he gave it to us in the form of a meal we share together. The individualist claims, "I can worship God quite well by myself," but to me, that's like saying "I can celebrate a birthday quite well by myself," or even, "I don't need to eat with the rest of my family." Corporate worship—on Sunday or any other day—is something the Christian family does *together*.

Corporate worship takes many different forms across the spectrum of Christian traditions. In my own Anglican tradition we use a written form of service based on a traditional outline. It includes hymns and prayers, scripture readings and a sermon, confession of sin, and sharing the bread and wine of Holy Communion. But I also enjoy visiting other churches with a less formal style of worship and more contemporary music, and I have been especially blessed by a local Mennonite church where the congregation often sings together in wonderful four-part harmony. I don't see these different traditions as being in competition with each other. I prefer to see all of them as having good things to share with the wider Christian family.

I find it important to remind myself regularly that the focus of worship is meant to be on God, not myself and my own likes and dislikes. For people who are new to Christianity, going to church for the first time can feel like attending a concert or play: an audience sitting in rows, facing a raised platform on which people in formal dress give speeches, perform rituals, and lead songs. To newcomers it can feel like a performance, and the temptation is to judge it on the basis of its entertainment value.

But that's not the point. When I attend a church service I'm not a member of the audience; I'm one of the performers. The pastor or minister isn't a soloist; she's more like a conductor, and we're all members of the orchestra under her direction, joining together in an act of worship to express our love and admiration for the Creator of the universe. Christian worship should help us fix our minds and hearts on God and encourage us to carry that focus with us as we go into the week ahead.

So corporate worship is important to us, but we can also benefit from a further discipline: **small group fellowship**. One reason for this is that many congregations are too big for people to really get to know one another, and even smaller ones aren't necessarily much better, because the Sunday morning culture is too formal.

I was first introduced to the power of small groups when I was a teenager. I made a commitment to Christ at the age of thirteen, and over the next few years our church started a number of 'home groups,' as we called them in those days. Some met in the evening, some in the afternoon. The content varied, but they all tended to include group Bible study, prayer, and singing. Crucially, there was opportunity for the participants to get to know one another and support each other on the Christian journey.

I eventually settled down as a member of the Thursday night group that met at the home of Ken and Kath. I am not exaggerating when I say that Thursdays were the best day of my week because of that group. I can remember sitting in a high school science class on a Thursday afternoon, thinking to myself, "Tonight's the night!"

In my present parish I'm a member of a Bible study group that meets at eight o'clock on Thursday mornings. We used to meet at a local coffee shop, but when the Covid-19 pandemic struck, we moved our meetings online. One unexpected side benefit has been that a former member, who moved several years ago to a different city, has been able to come back to our group. He once said something that really struck me: "When I lived in Edmonton, this group was the highlight of my week." When I heard those words, I remembered how I felt about that Thursday night home group when I was a teenager, and I smiled to myself. Even in our busy modern world, small group fellowship is as valuable as ever.

When I look around at the Christians I know who are growing steadily in their faith, the vast majority are involved in a small group for Bible study, prayer, and support. In such a group we can get to know one another, and we can share our struggles and doubts with people who care for us. We can discuss the scriptures and hear how God is using them to speak to others. We can pray for each other and ask for prayers for ourselves.

~

A New Way of Living

In Matthew 6:33 Jesus says, "But seek first the kingdom of God and his righteousness, and all these things will be given to you as well." Christians believe the world will only find its deepest needs fulfilled when the will of God is done perfectly on earth as in heaven. So we set ourselves to learn and do the will of God, in our personal lives, our families, our work, and every other area of our world. And because we believe God has been revealed to us in Jesus, we make it our priority to learn to see life as Jesus sees it, and to live life as he taught it.

This is going to be a struggle for us. It involves unlearning some ways of thinking and acting, and learning new ways that seem strange and unfamiliar to us. Here are some examples.

This new way of living will affect **our priorities.** When we say, "Jesus is my Lord," one of the things we're saying is "I will let Jesus teach me what my priorities should be." These days there are many others claiming that right: our employers, our friends, the media, society in general, to name just a few. To live as a follower of Jesus will mean that getting to know God and spreading God's kingdom will come first for us, and we'll look for God's guidance as we consider our other priorities.

This new way of living will affect **our view of success.** To many people, success is defined by getting a good job, achieving a high standard of living, and being respected and liked by your peers. But Jesus had a different view. He said, "You shall love the Lord your God with all your heart, and with all your soul, and with all your mind, and with all your strength...You shall love your neighbour as yourself" (Mark 12:30-31). If you can learn to live like that, then Jesus sees you as a successful person. On the other hand, if you get ahead in life and make a lot of money, but fail to learn this life of love, then you've missed the whole point.

This leads us to the next thing: this new way of living will affect **our view of money and possessions**. They're probably the number one false god in modern society; people look to them for happiness, for security and meaning in life. Many Christians are trying to have the best of both worlds here and causing themselves endless trouble by doing so. I believe consistent

Christians will always be poorer than their neighbours, for two reasons: first, they'll be finding their happiness in something other than money and possessions, and second, they'll be having so much fun learning to give to those who are in need.

The next point: this new way of life is going to affect **our view of the poor and needy**. In 1996 when the Atlanta Olympics were about to begin, the local police swept all the homeless off the streets and banished them from the city for the duration of the games. Clearly, the poor were seen as an embarrassment. But to followers of Jesus the poor and needy aren't an embarrassment; they're an opportunity to serve God. In Matthew chapter 25 we're told that when we feed the hungry, clothe the naked, visit the sick or prisoners, or help others in need, it's really Jesus we're helping. We love God by loving the people God loves.

There is one more area I need to mention, because the Christian view on it is so different to the prevalent view in our world. This new way of living will affect **our view of our enemies.**

In *The Complete Book of Running,* Jim Fixx told a story about a solitary jogger who was heckled by a carload of teenagers. The car sped off down the road, but the jogger overtook it at a traffic light. Holding a steady pace, he ran right over the car – one heavy step on the trunk, one on the roof, one on the hood – leaving three great dents. He then took off down a side street, and by the time the light changed he was long gone.

Yes, it's a hilarious story (and according to Fixx, the group who first heard it responded with a standing ovation), but if you think about it for a moment, it's also problematic. Most runners have been heckled from time to time, and have probably fantasized about vengeance, but in our modern world vengeance is a huge problem, because it escalates, and it never ends. You hit me, I'll hit you back harder, then you'll hit me back again, and so it continues. You burn down my village, I'll burn down ten of yours. This is the way the world works.

Jesus' way of life was totally different. Instead of responding to hatred with hatred, he absorbed the hatred and violence and responded with love. When he was crucified, he prayed for his enemies: "Father, forgive them, for they do not know what they are doing" (Luke 23.34). And he taught his followers to do the same: to turn the other cheek and love their enemies. Paul spells it out for us:

> 'Instead, "if your enemies are hungry, feed them; if they are thirsty, give them something to drink; for by doing this you will heap burning coals on their heads." Do not be overcome by evil, but overcome evil with good.' (Romans 12.20-21)

The New Testament writers make it clear that becoming a follower of Jesus involves a major rethink of how we treat the people we see as our enemies. I'm not exaggerating when I say that, for many, this will be the biggest challenge in learning the Christian way of life.

~

Conclusion

It might be helpful to think of the Christian life as a tree. The new way of living is the fruit on the tree: we're trying to grow Christian character, get our priorities right, live simply, care for the poor and needy, and love our neighbour as we love ourselves. But if we want the tree to be healthy, we'll also have to give attention to the roots, because they bring us nourishment from the soil around us. We receive that nourishment through our relationships with God and with the family of God, and the four disciplines we've talked about—prayer, Bible reading, communal worship, and small group fellowship—are some of the most important of those roots. If we're faithful in practicing those things, we'll receive the nourishment and strength we need to live the new life Jesus is teaching us.

What will be the result? Let me close with some verses from the New Testament letter to the Ephesians:

> 'When I think of all this, I fall to my knees and pray to the Father, the Creator of everything in heaven and on earth. I pray that from his glorious, unlimited resources he will empower you with inner strength through his Spirit. Then

Christ will make his home in your hearts as you trust in him. Your roots will grow down into God's love and keep you strong. And may you have the power to understand, as all God's people should, how wide, how long, how high, and how deep his love is. May you experience the love of Christ, though it is too great to understand fully. Then you will be made complete with all the fullness of life and power that comes from God.' (Ephesians 3.14-19 NLT)

~

Sources

The three-heading structure of this chapter comes from a talk by Harold Percy.

The story by Max Lucado is found in his book *When God Whispers Your Name* (Dallas; Word Publishing; 1994), 145.

The story about the jogger who ran over a car is found in James F. Fixx, *The Complete Book of Running* (New York, Random House, 1977), 159.

CHAPTER 5:

LEARNING TO PRAY

I approach the subject of prayer with a certain amount of trepidation. St. Francis of Assisi said, "What a person is on their knees before God, that they are—and no more." Judged by that sentence, I know I am a very small person to be writing about prayer, because even after more than forty-five years of praying seriously, I still feel like a beginner.

As I said in the last chapter, the first real teaching I received on this subject came in the form of a little booklet my father gave me a few days after I had committed my life to Jesus. It was called *Seven Minutes with God,* and it was designed to help new Christians form the habit of daily prayer and Bible reading. Seven minutes doesn't sound very long, but it was a lot longer than the time I had been accustomed to spending in prayer up to that point. The book was very precise about amounts of time: half a minute in silence and opening prayer, four minutes in Bible reading, half a minute in praise, half a minute in thanksgiving, half a minute in confessing my sins, half a minute in asking for things for myself and others. It also explained very clearly and simply what those different parts of prayer were actually all about.

Not long after I read *Seven Minutes with God,* I started to use daily Bible reading notes put out by the Bible Reading Fellowship. They came in the form of a little booklet with a reading for each day, accompanied by explanatory comments to help the ordinary reader. I remember as a teenager getting up early in the morning to read my Bible reading notes and spend a few minutes in prayer over my breakfast cereal before I went out into the cold and damp English morning to do my paper route!

In this way, in those early days of my Christian life, I was helped to form a habit that has stayed with me now for over forty-five years—the habit of starting every day with God in prayer.

Aside from my ministry, about the only other thing I do really well is to play the guitar. People are sometimes kind enough to ask me, "How did you learn to play so well?" My answer is "one day at a time." I made a habit over many years of playing every day, and I also listened to records and played along with more experienced guitarists, trying to imitate what I saw them doing. Playing became a daily habit for me, and that's the entire secret of how I was able to develop my skills.

Prayer is a positive habit. Some people don't like calling it a habit; they're afraid of reducing prayer to a mindless routine. It seems to me that there are two equal and opposite errors we can fall into on that subject. Some people really stress the habit; it's almost as if they're saying, "I've got to pray now, whether I like it or not!" Their discipline is admirable, but they seem to have lost some of the joy and spontaneity of the psalm writers, who wrote as if they *loved* to be in the Lord's presence. On the other extreme, there are people who stress the spontaneity. They say, "I don't have to discipline myself to pray; I love it and I do it because I want to." That's also admirable, but if the only thing motivating you to pray is emotion, what will you do when the emotion just isn't there (which, sooner or later, will inevitably happen)? What we need is a balance between these two extremes.

~

Five Principles of Prayer

Jesus knows our need of help with prayer, and he has given us specific guidance on the subject in Matthew's Gospel:

> "And whenever you pray, do not be like the hypocrites; for they love to stand and pray in the synagogues and at the street corners, so that they may be seen by others. Truly I tell you, they have received their reward. But whenever you pray, go into your room and shut the door and pray to your Father who is in secret; and your Father who sees in secret will reward you.

"When you are praying, do not heap up empty phrases as the gentiles do; for they think that they will be heard because of their many words. Do not be like them, for your Father knows what you need before you ask him.

"Pray then in this way:

> "Our Father in heaven,
> May your name be revered as holy.
> May your kingdom come.
> May your will be done,
> on earth as it is in heaven.
> Give us today our daily bread.
> And forgive us our debts,
> as we also have forgiven our debtors.
> And do not bring us to the time of trial,
> but rescue us from the evil one." (Matthew 6.5-13)

In this passage we can see five principles about prayer:

~

Pray regularly

Notice that in Matthew 6.7 Jesus doesn't say *"If* you pray," but *"When* you pray." He assumed we would make prayer a habitual part of our lives. Jesus was raised as a godly Jew and would have known the book of Psalms in the Hebrew scriptures almost by heart. In Psalm 5:3 the writer says, 'O Lord, in the morning you hear my voice; in the morning I plead my case to you and watch.' We saw in the last chapter that Jesus followed this same pattern himself. Mark tells us that 'Early in the morning, well before sunrise, Jesus rose and went to a deserted place where he could be alone in prayer' (Mark 1:35 CEB). If Jesus, the Son of God, needed to pray in order to maintain his relationship with his Father in heaven, how much more do we, his followers, also need regular prayer?

Some people say, "I can pray all day long—I don't need a specific time of prayer." I definitely believe there are people who can do this; I'm married to one of them. However, I also believe that most of us aren't as good at this as we would like to think.

For most of us, having a specific time of prayer each day *helps* us pray all day long. So I think most would benefit from finding a time and place to pray and getting into a habit.

~

Pray in a habitual place

When Jesus says "...go into your room and shut the door and pray to your Father who is in secret" (Matthew 6.6), he isn't saying it's wrong to pray together with other Christians. The context shows that he was worried about people showing off their spirituality by praying their private prayers in full view of other people. He was saying, "This is between you and God. Don't pray with one eye on your audience; pray out of a sincere desire to get closer to God."

Most of the people to whom Jesus was speaking wouldn't actually have had rooms of their own, so they wouldn't have been able to obey him literally. Most Galilean peasants lived in one-room houses shared not only with other family members but animals as well. No doubt that's why Jesus got up so early and left the town when he wanted to pray. Like him, many people today still find going for a solitary walk a good way to make time and space for prayer.

A well-known writer and speaker once remarked that the people he knew who prayed the most consistently could usually describe to him the physical environment in which they prayed. I think that would be true for me, too. I know people who write their prayers in notebooks in coffee shops; they sit in the same seat at the same table every day. I know people who have particular chairs in their living rooms where they like to sit in the quiet to read their Bibles and pray. I have clergy friends who kneel in the same pew in their churches each day to say their prayers.

In one of my parishes I had a chair in my office that was like a sanctuary for me, because it was the place I always prayed. C.S. Lewis tells of a man who enjoyed praying in railway carriages; he said they provided exactly the right combination of quiet and distraction. Any place can become a place of prayer for us, but if we want to remember to pray daily, most people find it helpful to establish a particular place and a particular time for their meetings with God.

~

Pray together if you can

One thing we often miss about the Lord's Prayer is that all the pronouns are plural. "*Our* Father in heaven...Give *us* today *our* daily bread. And forgive *us our* debts, as *we* also have forgiven *our* debtors. And do not bring *us* to the time of trial, but rescue *us* from the evil one" (Matthew 6.9, 11-13). This isn't phrased as a prayer an individual prays alone. The default setting is that followers of Jesus will pray this prayer together.

Many of us are familiar with the corporate use of this prayer as part of a formal church worship service, and some of us will also be in the habit of using it as part of our personal prayers. But I suspect that very few of us nowadays will use it in small group settings during the week. When we think about prayer during the week, most of us think about private prayer, when we're alone with God.

Jesus is not against such private prayer—we know from the Gospels that he practiced it himself—but we also know from the Book of Acts that the early Christians loved praying together. I would argue that if people in the Bible had the choice of praying alone or praying together, they would normally choose praying together. Even when we pray alone, if we use the Lord's Prayer we're not really praying alone. We're praying as part of a dispersed community.

Family prayer is a custom that used to be quite common; in fact, the 1959 Canadian *Book of Common Prayer* includes forms of daily prayer for use in families, perhaps at the end of a meal. If young children are present, we'll need to be creative about finding ways of praying that they'll enjoy, and fortunately for us, there are many resources available for this. Special seasons of the year are particularly good times for this; I think of Advent, for instance, when the family can light the candles of an Advent wreath together and pray prayers appropriate to the season.

Prayer together can be especially helpful for couples. The forms I'll describe in a few minutes don't require praying alone;

it can be a very meaningful experience for a couple to pray them together. If we're not married or otherwise attached, we can still seek out a Christian friend who will agree to pray with us regularly, perhaps once or twice a week.

Prayer alone will always be important, and for most of us it will probably be our most common way of praying during the week. But if we have the opportunity to pray regularly with someone else, we should seize it with both hands. A commitment to pray together helps keep us steady in our prayer life, and it can also bring a new level of honesty and openness into our relationships with one another.

~

Pray sincerely

Jesus says, "When you are praying, do not heap up empty phrases as the gentiles do" (Matthew 6.7), or, as one version of the Bible says, "Do not go babbling on like the heathen!"

It's important to Jesus that we mean what we say when we pray. I'm an Anglican, and I sometimes think that for Anglicans the beauty of our liturgy can be a snare to us; it intimidates us into thinking we have to phrase all our prayers beautifully. But in the Lord's Prayer, Jesus gives us a very simple model.

Whether you pray using your own words or the words of someone else, after a while you'll find it easy to say words without thinking what they mean. I once heard a story of a prayer group in which one of the members always used the phrase "Lord, sweep the cobwebs from our hearts." The other members of the group got tired of this, and finally one night at the end of this man's prayer, someone else chimed in, "And, Lord, please shoot that spider!"

If you want examples of prayers that come straight from the heart, look at the book of Psalms in the Bible. It's a collection of prayers written in the centuries before the time of Jesus, and prayer from the heart is what the writers specialise in. Psalm 62:8 says 'Trust in him at all times, O people; pour out your heart before him; God is a refuge for us.' Eugene Peterson has produced a paraphrase of the Bible, *The Message,* which is especially vivid in places. It really brings out the heartfelt quality of the psalms. Here is Psalm 6 from *The Message:*

> Please, GOD, no more yelling,
>   no more trips to the woodshed.
> Treat me nice for a change;
>   I'm so starving for affection.
>
> Can't you see I'm black and blue,
>   beat up badly in bones and soul?
> GOD, how long will it take
>   for you to let up?
>
> Break in, GOD, and break up this fight;
>   if you love me at all, get me out of here.
> I'm no good to you dead, am I?
>   I can't sing in your choir if I'm buried in some tomb!
>
> I'm tired of all this—so tired. My bed
>   has been flooded forty days and nights
> on the flood of my tears.
>   My mattress is soaked, soggy with tears.
> The sockets of my eyes are black holes;
>   nearly blind, I squint and grope.
>
> Get out of here, you Devil's crew
>   at last GOD has heard my sobs.
> My requests have all been granted,
>   my prayers are answered.
>
> Cowards, my enemies disappear.
> Disgraced, they turn tail and run.

That is a wonderful example of a prayer from the heart.

~

Pray specifically

The Lord's Prayer is a no-nonsense, get-specific list of prayer requests to God. Notice that these are not self-centred prayer requests. In fact, when we pray the Lord's Prayer we don't start with our own concerns at all, but with God's concerns. The Lord's Prayer includes worship ('may your name be revered as holy'), requests for God's concerns ('Your kingdom come. Your will be done') and our own concerns ('Give us today our daily bread'). It includes confession and forgiveness ('forgive us our debts') and a request for spiritual help ('rescue us from the evil one').

When Jesus gave us this prayer he didn't intend that we just recite it in our public worship, although it is quite acceptable to do that. He also gave it to us as a framework on which we can hang our own prayers. When someone once asked St. Teresa of Avila how to pray, her response was "Pray the Lord's Prayer, but take an hour to do it." That's a little intimidating for me—an hour of prayer is very difficult—but I have found that after a few years of practice I can do it for fifteen minutes.

~

Putting the Principles into Practice

How do we go about putting all this into practice? Let me share with you three ways in which Christians down through the years have applied these prayer principles.

~

Prayer using our own words

This is sometimes called 'extemporary prayer.' When I was a student at the Church Army Training College in Toronto there was a lot of emphasis on this method of prayer. I was taught to have a daily quiet time which combined prayer and Bible reading. It worked like this.

I would start with Bible reading. I was using Bible reading notes which would give me a scripture passage for each day, so I would read the passage and then the explanations in the notes. I would then think about what I had read and try to write down one important lesson, what one of my teachers called 'a best thought for the day.'

I would then turn to prayer. My prayers were very informal and followed a little acronym which I used for a pattern: the word ACTS. 'A' stood for 'Adoration,' prayers of worship and praise to God. 'C' stood for 'Confession,' when I would mention specific sins and ask God's forgiveness for them. 'T' stood for 'Thanksgiving,' and I tried to be as specific as possible about the things I gave thanks for. 'S' stood for 'Supplication,' asking for things, mainly for others but also for myself. The model I used in the last chapter, when I said that everything I needed to know about prayer I learned in kindergarten, is a new variation on this ACTS pattern.

~

Prayer using other people's words

We all have times when we don't know how we ought to pray, and in those times it's often helpful to look at the prayers people have prayed before us. In Christianity we have a long tradition of taking the words of others and making them our own in prayer. The oldest example of this is the book of *Psalms*, which I mentioned earlier. This collection of prayers and hymns was created by people in the centuries before the time of Jesus. Some of the psalms were written to be used in public worship, while others are obviously private prayers. There are 150 of them, and they run through the whole range of human emotions and experiences. They are a wonderful model for our own prayers.

Like many other Christians, Anglicans have an old tradition of using services of 'Morning Prayer' and 'Evening Prayer' as a framework for daily prayer. These services were originally created by monks and nuns, but they can be very helpful for ordinary Christians.

There are many different versions of Morning and Evening Prayer, but there are some things they have in common. Most include a daily 'lectionary' or list of Bible readings for the whole year; they also include selections from the psalms and other biblical hymns and songs, and other prayers with a long history in the Christian tradition. One such prayer that I particularly enjoy is found originally in the *Book of Common Prayer*; but I quote it here in the version in the *Book of Alternative Services:*

> Lord God, almighty and everlasting Father, you have brought us in safety to this new day. Preserve us with your mighty power, that we may not fall into sin, or be overcome by adversity; and in all we do, direct us to the

fulfilling of your purpose; through Jesus Christ our Lord. Amen.

I find it very easy to put my own meaning into the words of that prayer. For instance, it's not hard for me to think of sins or adversities I want God to help me avoid during the day.

You'll notice that these prayers are written in the plural rather than singular form. Some people find this a problem, but personally I find it helpful; it reminds me of all the others around the world praying with me as I use these prayers. And of course, the plural form is particularly helpful if we're praying together with others.

I suspect that most people who pray use a combination of these first two methods. People who mainly use their own words will often include the Lord's Prayer, and people who use daily Morning and Evening Prayer usually build in a time for their own concerns and requests. But alongside these two ways of praying there is a third, which is also important.

~

Prayer using no words

There was once an old man who made a habit of sitting quietly in a church every day for extended periods of time, simply looking at the crucifix. The parish priest noticed this, and one day he sat down beside the old man and said "You seem to spend a lot of time in prayer every day. What are you praying about?" The old man replied, "Nothing." Then, pointing at the crucifix, he said, "I look at him, and he looks at me, and we are happy together."

We don't always have to be talking when we pray. After all, when we really get to know someone, we're comfortable being silent in their presence. In the same way, it's good sometimes for us to sit quietly and enjoy the fact that God is with us. There are times when, if we're quiet long enough, we'll hear God speaking to us in the silence. We won't usually hear an audible voice. We may just have a sense that God is speaking to us, with a message addressed directly to our situation.

Some Christian traditions have developed disciplines to help people pray silently in this way. For instance, some try to keep a word in their mind to help them concentrate—perhaps the name of Jesus, or another prayer word or phrase such as 'Lord, have mercy,' or 'maranatha' (an Aramaic prayer meaning 'Come, Lord Jesus'). Others will concentrate on their breathing, and imagine they are inhaling God's love into the depths of their soul. Personally, I sometimes find that just lighting a candle and sitting quietly with it for a few minutes helps me focus on God.

So here are three ways to apply the principles of prayer to our daily lives. We can pray using our own words, we can pray using the words of other people, and we can pray using no words at all. A balanced prayer life would include all three of these, although most of us will probably find that one of them becomes our favourite.

~

Conclusion

Prayer isn't easy. It's a habit we haven't been taught in our culture, so we shouldn't be surprised if it takes a while for us to learn the basic skills we need. But if we keep practising, prayer can become a daily lifeline for us. In prayer we connect with God, and we put ourselves in the place where God can bring us the peace, the strength, the comfort, and even the challenge, that we need at any given time. Prayer can be an adventure. I encourage you to persevere in it.

~

Sources

C.S. Lewis' story about the man who enjoyed praying in railway carriages is found in his book *Letters to Malcolm: Chiefly on Prayer* (London; Geoffrey Bles Ltd.; 1964), 30.

The prayer from Morning Prayer is from *The Book of Alternative Services of the Anglican Church of Canada* (Toronto; Anglican Book Centre; 1985), 131.

CHAPTER 6:

USING THE BIBLE

Many years ago now, a man in one of my churches heard me preach a sermon about the importance of reading the Bible. He was a typical Anglican, in that he came to church regularly and heard passages of the Bible read aloud, but he very rarely dipped into it for himself. But something clicked for him when he heard my sermon, and he decided to try reading the Bible all the way through.

He had a copy of the *Good News Bible,* a modern translation, and he decided to start from the beginning (the book of Genesis) and read through to the end (the book of Revelation). He read for fifteen minutes every night, right before bed, and it took him about eight months to make it to the end.

I need to say that I was impressed with him for sticking with it! Many people start reading the Bible straight through, but most of them get discouraged and give up in Exodus or Leviticus. My friend made it through to the end, but he found it more challenging than he'd expected.

We went for coffee when he was about halfway through, and he told me he was finding it hard going. "I have to confess," he said, "it's not what I was expecting."

"Oh?" I replied. "How so?"

"I thought it would be full of inspiring stories about good and holy people, but it's not like that. It's full of wars and battles and people killing each other, and thousands of animals being slaughtered in sacrifice. Why would God make all those lovely animals and then ask people to kill them to show how much they love him? And most people in the Bible aren't very moral! They lie and trick each other, and have long feuds, and they're so savage and cruel! And God tells them to start wars and wipe out whole populations." He shook his head slowly. "I honestly don't know if I can stick with it."

I don't remember exactly what I said but it was probably something like this. "Remember, the Bible is full of stories about people just like us. We often mess things up. Sometimes we think God wants us to do something, but later, we realize we were probably wrong about that. Still, we keep trying to grow and learn, and God never gives up on us. We may not be perfect, but God doesn't have any perfect people to work with. He's only got us!"

~

When I was a child I was like my friend; I encountered the Bible in church, or in Bible story books my parents read to me. I was familiar with some of the stories, but I was hazy about the timeline. I realize now that I was totally unaware of huge portions of the Bible, including the Old Testament laws, the history of the Israelite monarchy, and most of the prophets.

In those days most people still read the Bible in the King James Version (KJV). It was first published in 1611, and some of the language in it was archaic even then. The wording was difficult to understand, and even though I loved reading, I was rarely tempted to try it.

However, I was fortunate that in the early 1970s a number of excellent modern versions of the Bible were starting to be published. The *New English Bible* came out in 1970, and I did some reading in it, but the version that really made me into a Bible reader was the *Living Bible*. This was a paraphrase produced by an American pastor, Ken Taylor. He set out to make it easy for modern people to understand the sense of the original Hebrew and Greek texts, but he didn't feel compelled to give a strictly literal rendering. Nowadays I don't recommend the *Living Bible* because some of its translations are actually misleading, but I'll always be grateful that it got me started. It was the first version of the Bible I read right through from cover to cover.

As I look back on that first reading experience, one thing that stands out for me was how rarely I was bothered by controversies about whether or not every word of the Bible was literally true. Instinctively, without ever having a conversation with anyone on the subject, I sensed that some of the stories might not be historically accurate, but they were still God-given stories with important things to teach me. Somehow I was able to avoid getting ambushed by difficult passages; I was able to see them against the backdrop of the bigger story the Bible was telling, the story of God's love for the people God had created.

As I mentioned in the last chapter, I was also helped by the fact that my dad introduced me very quickly to Bible reading notes. Reading a library of books written over two thousand years ago is challenging. Very few of us try to do it with any book other than the Bible, and if we do (with Plato or Aristotle, for instance), we usually have the help of scholars who've studied the background and can help us with difficult passages. For me, Bible reading notes were scholarship made accessible in bite-sized portions. Even now, many years later, I'm still grateful for the things I learned from them.

~

Not everyone's first experience of the Bible is as positive as mine.

A while back I was teaching a 'Christian Basics' course, and a young woman came to me during one of the coffee breaks to talk about the Bible. "That book has done so much damage to people," she said. I knew where she was coming from. She was a lesbian, and she'd been told over and over again that the Bible condemned people like her. In her mind, the seven verses that appear to condemn homosexuality spoke more loudly than the hundreds of verses about caring for the poor and needy and building a society of compassion and justice. It makes sense that she would see it that way: those verses addressed her deepest sense of who she was, and they told her she was unworthy of God's love.

I've talked to many people who were raised in churches with a strict fundamentalist understanding of the Bible. They've been taught that everything stated in the Bible is literal truth, even if it seems to contradict the findings of modern science. Many of these young people have gone on to study science and history, and sure enough, they've found things there that seem to contradict the Bible. This troubles them.

The problem is, they've only been taught one way of understanding the Bible. They've been taught that are only two options: accept the whole Bible as literal truth or accept the findings of modern science. In far too many cases, the result is sadly predictable: they not only abandon the Bible; they also abandon their whole heritage of faith in God, because it was so firmly tied to fundamentalism.

On the other end of the scale, there are also people who've been overwhelmed by all the opinions of modern scholarship and have lost all hope that the Bible can speak to them. I once heard Harold Percy talk about the experience so many of us had the first time we went on camping trips with the scouts or the guides. Our parents gave us flashlights to take with us, and being kids, the first thing we did was to take the flashlights apart. Inevitably, some of us found it difficult to put them back together, and the result was that when we got up in the night to go to the bathroom, we didn't have anything to shine a light on our path.

Many people have a similar experience with biblical scholarship. The scholars have the best of intentions, but the message people hear is that ordinary folks can't understand the Bible for themselves; they should leave it to people with degrees in biblical studies. As a result, ordinary people have been without the light the Bible could have given them as they tried to find their way in God's world.

I have an enormous appreciation for the insights of modern biblical scholarship, but I don't think most people realize how accessible it actually is. I often tell my parishioners that if they're willing to spend sixty dollars on a decent study Bible—a Bible with explanatory notes written by people who know what they're talking about—they'll have easy access to all the scholarship they need to give them a good understanding of the biblical texts.

~

Approaching the Bible

How are we to approach this book which has been so important in the lives of Christians for two thousand years?

Sometimes people talk about the Bible as a sort of manual for living. When you're wondering how to raise your children, or deal with sickness, or pray better, or understand the character of God, you should turn to the Bible for the guidance you're looking for.

I think there's some truth in that (though it's not as easy to access as it sounds, because the Bible isn't laid out thematically), but it's not where I'd start. I'd prefer to begin by talking about the Bible as *the story of God's love.* Yes, it gives us guidance about living, but it does so in the context of a grand narrative: the story of God's relationship with the world God made and the people God placed in it. And as we saw in chapter one, stories have the power to form us and shape us. We find out who we are, and what we're here for, in the context of the story of God's love.

~

The biblical library

One thing we need to remember is that the Bible isn't really a book at all: it's a *library* of books.

Depending on whether you follow the Protestant or the Catholic lists, there are either 66 or 82 books in the biblical library (more about this difference in a minute). As soon as we examine these books closely, we realize that this is one of the most extraordinary libraries we've ever entered.

To begin with, the various books were written over such a long time period. It's safe to say that some of the stories in the Old Testament must originate from at least 1000 BCE and possibly earlier. If the last books of the New Testament were written between 95-100 CE, that gives us a period of at least eleven hundred years over which these books were being written.

The books were written in different languages, and in cultures very different from ours. They include law, history, inspirational fiction, poetry, hymns and songs, biographies, letters, prophecies, and sermons. Obviously if we walked into our local library and picked up a biography, a book of poetry and a copy of the criminal code, we would approach each book very differently. And yet people often make the mistake of treating every part of the Bible as if it was exactly the same kind of writing.

Our Biblical library has two floors. The ground floor is the Hebrew Scriptures or Old Testament, and upstairs we find the New Testament. Some Bibles also contain a kind of stairwell between the floors, which we call either the Apocrypha or the Deuterocanonical books.

The Old Testament (sometimes called the First Testament or the Hebrew Scriptures) was written in Hebrew and a little Aramaic; it's mainly the story of God's dealings with the nation of Israel. It talks about how, around 1850 BCE, God called Abraham and led him to leave his home in Mesopotamia and move to a new land, which we now call Israel or Palestine. God's purpose, he told Abraham, was that "in you all the families of the earth shall be blessed" (Genesis 12:3).

Four hundred years later the Israelites were slaves in Egypt. God sent Moses to lead them out to their promised land, and in a famous series of supernatural events (beginning with the ten plagues and ending with the crossing of the Red Sea), God set them free from the Egyptians. Their journey wasn't exactly trouble-free; they were stubborn and hard-hearted and often refused to listen to God's guidance, and as a result, a trip that should have taken them a couple of weeks ended up taking forty years. I won't give the plot away—you can read it for yourself.

Moses is also associated with the Law, or 'Torah' (a Hebrew word that might be better translated as 'instruction'), which takes up the second half of the book of Exodus and large portions of the books of Leviticus, Numbers, and Deuteronomy. It includes not only the Ten Commandments and other moral laws, but also instructions about worship at the sanctuary, and detailed guidance for the judges of ancient Israel. Some of its laws may go back to the time of Moses, but most modern scholars believe that later generations built on Moses' work, adapting what he had written and adding new instructions to guide the community in its new situation in the promised land. Such was their respect for Moses, however, that the entire collection came to be known as 'the Torah of Moses.'

Sometime between 1000 and 900 BCE Saul became the first king of Israel, and he was followed by David, the famous shepherd boy who killed the giant Goliath. As an adult, David was probably Israel's greatest king. After the death of his son Solomon, the nation split into two: the southern kingdom of Judah and the northern kingdom of Israel. The books of Kings and Chronicles tell the sad story of their rebellion against God, to the point that eventually both nations were occupied by foreign armies and many of their people were deported. These deportations took place around 728 BCE for Israel, and 597 BCE for Judah. A generation or two later, exiles from Judah found their way back to Jerusalem, rebuilt their fallen temple and restored their nation. Shortly after this period the Old Testament history ends.

But before we go on, we need to mention that during the time of the kings of Israel and Judah, a devoted group of people were constantly trying to bring the nation back to God's plan. These were the prophets—people like Isaiah, Jeremiah, Amos, Micah, and many others like them, some of whom have books in the Hebrew scriptures named after them. These books are hard for us to understand, because they're mainly collections of sermons preached by these prophets, referring to specific events in the history of Israel. A good study Bible with footnotes can often help us identify those events, so we can have a greater understanding of the prophets' message.

The Hebrew scriptures also include 'wisdom literature'—poems and proverbs and meditations on the human condition. The psalms—the hymn book of ancient Israel—are part of this literature, but it also includes the books of Proverbs (a collection of wise sayings), Ecclesiastes (a meditation on the meaning of life), and Job (an examination of the question of why bad things happen to good people).

The New Testament, in contrast to the Hebrew scriptures, was written over a much shorter period of time. It was written in

Greek, which was the common language in the Mediterranean world in those days (like English in the world today). The person of Jesus dominates the New Testament, but he wrote no book. After his resurrection and ascension his apostles passed down the stories about him by word of mouth, which was more reliable in those days than it is now, because books were rare, and therefore people's memories were much better.

The first documents of the New Testament to be written were the letters the apostles (Paul, Peter, and others) wrote to churches they had founded or individuals they were working with. These letters were often written in answer to specific problems the churches were facing, and with a bit of reading between the lines we can often make a guess as to what those problems were.

As time went by the apostles began to die, and that was probably the impetus for the church to look toward written records of Jesus' life and teaching. The first person to write an account of the life of Jesus was probably Mark; we're told in a very early Christian tradition that he was a companion of Peter and wrote down the old apostle's reminiscences of Jesus. He was followed by Luke, Matthew, and then John. Luke also probably wrote the book of Acts, which tells stories of the early church from the end of Jesus' time on earth until Paul's imprisonment in Rome some thirty years later. The last book of the New Testament to be written was Revelation, a fascinating book which uses symbolic language to examine the whole sweep of human history, but is probably not the best place to start your study of the New Testament.

The Apocrypha, or Deuterocanonical books, is a collection of books written mainly after the time of the Hebrew Bible. When the Hebrew scriptures were translated into Greek before the time of Christ, these books were included in that translation, but for most of them there are no surviving Hebrew manuscripts. When the Jewish canon of scripture was settled in about 90 CE, these books were not included.

There has always been a disagreement in the church as to the status of these books. Roman Catholic and Eastern Orthodox Christians see them as part of the Hebrew scriptures, and in their

Bibles these books are interspersed with the other Old Testament documents. Protestant Christians follow the Jewish canon, so their Bibles don't include the Apocrypha. A third arrangement, dating back to the sixteenth century, is to include them in printed Bibles but gather them together in a separate section between the Old and New Testaments. Some editions of the Bible used in Anglican and other mainline churches follow this arrangement.

Nowadays, even though disagreement about their status continues, many Christians still find it profitable to read the books of the Apocrypha. The books of Maccabees tell stories of Jewish heroes who defended their nation in the second century BCE when a Greek tyrant was trying to wipe out their religion. Books like Sirach and the Wisdom of Solomon are similar to the Old Testament book of Proverbs, while Tobit and Judith are short stories like the books of Ruth and Esther. Paul sometimes alludes to the books of the Apocrypha in his letters, and he was clearly familiar with them.

~

Understanding the Library

The Christian Church has historically taken a very high view of the Bible. We see it as inspired by God, so that in some sense its words can convey the Word of God to us. We can see why this would be so.

~

The story the Bible tells is a unique story

Israel had a special place in God's plan for the world, and this story came to its climax in the visit God made to this planet in the person of Jesus. Christians believe that Jesus is the unique Son of God, and if that's true, it makes sense that the story of his life, death and resurrection, and the events that led up to it and followed it, would be the most important story in the history of this planet.

~

The people who wrote the Bible were unique people

In one sense, of course, they were ordinary people like you and me, who struggled with weaknesses and problems similar to our own. But they were also people who had been uniquely authorised to speak in God's name. The Hebrew prophets were certainly aware of this, and the New Testament apostles were given a commission by Jesus to pass on his teaching to his people. Jesus promised them the help of the Holy Spirit in this task. He said to them, "But the Advocate, the Holy Spirit, whom the Father will send in my name, will teach you everything and remind you of all that I have said to you" (John 14:26).

So we're justified in treating the scriptures with respect, but we also need to take their human authors seriously. Most Christians don't believe the Holy Spirit simply dictated the words of the Bible to the writers; the Bible itself contradicts this idea. For instance, Luke is very clear about the methods he used to write his gospel:

> Since many have undertaken to compile a narrative about the events that have been fulfilled among us, just as they were handed on to us by those who from the beginning were eyewitnesses and servants of the word, I too decided, as one having a grasp of everything from the start, to write a well-ordered account for you' (Luke 1:1-3a).

In other words, Luke was familiar with the story of Jesus, but he also consulted others. He wasn't an eyewitness, but he had easy access to the accounts of eyewitnesses who had told their stories before him. This would often have happened in the context of gatherings full of people who had known Jesus themselves.

How should we read this collection of books which are definitely the product of human creativity, but also claim to be inspired by the Holy Spirit? Let me answer that question with two phrases that may sound contradictory.

First, **read the Bible as you would read any other book.** In other words, we use our common sense and treat it as we would treat any other book written in the ancient world. We learn all we can about the culture and background of the people who wrote it. We consult the writings of people who have given their lives to studying it. We don't just dip into it, reading bits taken from here, there, and everywhere, and still expect it somehow to make sense. We approach it in an orderly fashion. If we've never read the Bible seriously before, that probably means, for instance, that before we study the Gospel of Luke we first read it all the way through to get the big picture. Then, when we come to study short passages of Luke, we'll have a better sense of how they fit into the whole book.

Second, **read the Bible as you read no other book.** No, I'm not contradicting myself here!

Let me give you an illustration. In some ways, Christians treat the bread of Holy Communion just like any other bread. For instance, when I as the pastor am preparing to handle it, I make sure my hands are clean so I don't pass on any disease to the members of my congregation. And the process by which our bodies receive this bread—tasting, chewing, swallowing, and digesting—is the same process as with any other food.

But there's another sense in which we treat this bread very differently from any other bread. God has promised us that if we receive it with faith in Jesus, we'll be fed by the Body and Blood of Jesus. This bread is a sacrament—an outward and visible sign of something inward and spiritual. It's ordinary physical bread, but it's also a means by which we receive the Bread of Heaven, Jesus himself.

The situation is similar with the Bible. Because it's a human book we prepare to read it as we prepare to read any other human book. But because it's been inspired by the Holy Spirit, we also treat it as we treat no other human book, believing that when we come to it with hearts full of faith in Jesus, God will still speak to us through its pages.

If we combine these two approaches—the common-sense human reading, and the expectant reading with faith in Christ—we'll be in a good position to receive the light and truth God wants to give us through the Bible. We'll be able to receive it as the writer of Psalm 119 received the Law of Moses, when he said, 'Your word is a lamp to my feet and a light to my path' (Psalm 119.105).

~

Using the Library

Reading with others

For the first fifteen hundred years of the history of the Christian Church, private Bible reading was impossible for most people, because they were illiterate. Also, the printing press hadn't been invented yet, so all books had to be copied out by hand, which made them far too expensive for most people to afford. This means that, for the majority of Christian history, coming together to hear the Bible read has been the norm, and for many people, this is still very helpful.

In recent years, all over the world, there's been an enormous explosion of small group Bible study. Whether we're talking about the smallest of small groups—a couple in their own home—or a group gathered in a church or coffee shop or even online, Christians are finding that when they meet regularly to open the Bible and discuss it together, their understanding takes enormous leaps and bounds. As I mentioned in chapter 4, in my own congregation I participate in an early morning Bible study group. After one of our meetings, a regular attendee said, "This group is where I get the most out of reading the Bible."

What happens in a Bible Study group? Typically, the leader or leaders will be using some sort of study guide, often a booklet with some background notes and some discussion questions to help the group members get at the meaning of the text. In many groups, each member will have a copy of the study guide and will be asked to do some preparation, reading over the Bible passage and the background materials, and thinking about the questions. When the group comes together, the members can listen and learn from each another.

What makes these groups so powerful is that each of us brings our own unique experience to our understanding of the text. This means that you might notice something I've missed, because your experience has prepared you to understand it better. I've been leading Bible study groups for over forty years, but I can honestly say that I often learn from the insights of group members who are relatively new to Bible reading. This is what makes these groups so worthwhile.

~

Reading alone

Reading and studying with others is helpful, but reading the Bible alone shouldn't be neglected. Let me suggest a couple of ways we can approach this.

We can read through a book. We don't necessarily have to do it in one sitting, although this is easier than many people think. A book like the Gospel of Mark can be read at home in one evening, and if you've never done it before, you'd probably find it unforgettable. I know of a small group that read the book of Revelation aloud in about an hour and a half.

Reading a book all the way through before we study its individual parts is a good way of getting the big picture. Books like Genesis, 1 and 2 Samuel, Matthew, or Acts are really good to read in this way. So are the New Testament letters, which were probably written to be read aloud at one sitting in meetings of house churches.

This doesn't apply to all the books in the library, though, and this is where we need to use our common sense. For instance, the book of Psalms is a book of hymns and poems, and we don't usually read that kind of book from cover to cover. That's why Martin Luther suggested taking the psalms one or two a day and using them as prayers if they seem appropriate to our situation.

We can meditate on a passage. The way we do this is to select a short section—perhaps from a book we've just read all the way through—and read it slowly and prayerfully, asking God to speak to us through the words of the passage.

Sometimes when we do this we won't have to work hard at all; something will leap right out at us, and we'll know it's meant especially for us today. But this doesn't always happen, so we need to use the minds God has given us to tease out God's message for us. We can do this by asking the passage some questions: Is there some wisdom or instruction here for me to listen to? Is there a good example for me to follow, or a bad example for me to avoid? Is there a promise for me to receive? Is there a new way of looking at the world for me to learn? Is there someone in this passage like me, and if so, what does Jesus say to them? These are just a few examples of helpful questions to bring to our meditation. Of course, we should also pray about what we're reading and ask God for greater understanding.

I've already mentioned daily Bible reading notes. These books or booklets give a passage of scripture to read each day, along with a short comment to explain the text and help us apply it to our lives. Many people find these notes very helpful. In these days of smart phones, many publishers have made their Bible reading notes available as apps; three that I can think of include Forward Day by Day, the Bible Reading Fellowship, and Our Daily Bread. A simple App Store search will soon locate them; some of them are available for free, and many can be sampled on the publisher's web site.

One last word about this process of meditating on scripture. Personally—and I know I'm not alone in this—I find it very helpful to write down the thoughts that come to me as I'm pondering and praying about the passage for the day. I'm not good at remembering things unless I write them down, and it also helps me be definite about what I think I'm hearing from God.

~

A word about translations of the Bible

Every English Bible we read is a translation from the original Hebrew, Aramaic and Greek. Also, we don't have an original manuscript of any book of the Bible; the oldest manuscripts we have are still copies. But, particularly with the New Testament, we have enough copies to be sure they're reasonably accurate.

Translations tend to vary between those that are highly literal on one hand, and those that are easy to read on the other. Literal translations are extremely accurate but often difficult to use. Examples of this kind of translation today are the *New American Standard Bible* (NASB) and the *English Standard Version* (ESV). At the other extreme we have paraphrases, which try so hard to be easy to read that they sometimes stray away from accuracy. The most widely used example of this kind of translation is *The Message*.

Most versions fall somewhere in the middle. The *New Revised Standard Version* (NRSV) is a very accurate translation and has recently (in 2021) been updated as the *New Revised Standard Version, Updated Edition* (NRSVue). The *New International Version* (NIV) is almost as accurate but quite a bit more readable (make sure you get the 2011 revision of the NIV, which is more accurate than earlier versions). There are a trio of translations that originate in Britain, and this is reflected in the style of English they use: the *New English Bible* (NEB) and its successor the *Revised English Bible* (REB), and the *New Jerusalem Bible* (NJB). If you are looking for something closer to the paraphrase end of the scale, you might want to look at *the Good News Translation* (GNT), the *New Living Translation* (NLT), or the *Common English Bible* (CEB). However, if you are studying a passage you should check them against the NRSV or NIV as sometimes the freer translations are less accurate.

Many translations of the Bible are available today in study Bible format. A study Bible has footnotes explaining obscure points in the passage, and it will often include introductions and maps. Some of the best of these are the *Cultural Backgrounds Study Bible* (available for the NIV and NRSV), the *New Oxford Annotated Bible* (for the NRSV), and the *CEB Study Bible* (for the CEB).

Bibles are available in all kinds of bindings, from cheap paperbacks to sturdy hardbacks to top grain leather costing a hundred dollars or even more. Only you can decide how much money you want to spend, although I will say that if you plan to use your Bible for a number of years, it's probably a good idea to spend a little more money and get a good hardback edition rather than a paperback that will fall apart after a few months.

~

Sources

The illustration of the Bible as a library of books with two floors comes from Harold Percy's book *Following Jesus: First Steps on the Way* (Toronto; Anglican Book Centre; 1993), 16.

CHAPTER 7:

THE FAMILY OF GOD

"I don't go to church, but you don't have to go to church to be a Christian."

I began my full-time ministry in the late 1970s, and even back then, this was a common phrase. In the years since then, it's become even more common, and recently its popularity has increased dramatically.

Some who use it were once church members but have now left. Many of them have had painful experiences with the institutional church or its individual members, and those experiences shouldn't be dismissed by defensive Christians. Others have been affected by the individualism of our times, or the growing skepticism about institutions, or the consumerism which has had a dramatic impact on the brand loyalty of previous generations.

So let's face this question head on: How important is it to belong to the church?

~

How Important is it to Belong to the Church?

The first thing I want to say is that, if we're taking our cue from the Bible, we'll look in vain for any example of a follower of Jesus who isn't part of a local church. The New Testament writers assume that Christians will meet together regularly for worship, prayer, learning, and mutual encouragement. One place where the issue is directly addressed is in the letter to the Hebrews:

> And let us not neglect our meeting together, as some people do, but encourage one another, especially now that the day of his return is drawing near. (Hebrews 10.25 NLT)

Let's go back to the beginning of the ministry of Jesus. According to the gospels, one of the first things he did was to call people to follow him. Those people weren't coming to him for individual lessons. Following Jesus was a group experience, and the new disciples had to learn not only to get along with him, but also with each other.

Given what we know about some of them, this wouldn't always have been easy. They were a group of ordinary, imperfect people, with very different backgrounds. One of them, Matthew, had been a tax collector, working either for the Roman government or the Galilean administration. Another, Simon, was identified as a Zealot; the Zealots were a terrorist organisation dedicated to the violent overthrow of the Roman administration. Can you imagine the campfire conversations between these two?

In other words, this wasn't a picture-perfect community where everyone just smiled and got along. The gospels tell us about rivalries, jealousies, and many instances when the disciples misunderstood what Jesus was saying to them. In the context of this flawed and imperfect community, they grew as followers of Jesus. Eventually Jesus sent them out to spread his message, and they did as he had done—preached the gospel, gathered people together into communities of disciples, and taught them how to follow Jesus.

Let me introduce you to one such community; it's the very first one the followers of Jesus started after he ascended into heaven. Here's how this community is described near the beginning of the book of Acts:

> So those who welcomed Peter's message were baptized, and that day about three thousand persons were added. They devoted themselves to the apostles' teaching and fellowship, to the breaking of bread and the prayers.
>
> Awe came upon everyone because many wonders and signs were being done through the apostles. All who believed were together and had all things in common; they would sell their possessions and goods and distribute the

> proceeds to all, as any had need. Day by day, as they spent much time together in the temple, they broke bread at home and ate their food with glad and generous hearts, praising God and having the goodwill of all the people. And day by day the Lord added to their number those who were being saved. (Acts 2.41-47).

We use the word 'church' a lot, but do we have a clear idea of what we mean by it? This passage can help us.

~

What is 'the Church'?

When we use the word 'church' today, the first thing that comes to mind is often some sort of building. So it might come as a surprise to us that some of the most effective outreach work in the history of the church was done in the first three centuries of its life, when the church had no buildings and very little institutional structure. When New Testament Christians talked about the church, they weren't referring to a building, but to a group of people. You didn't just 'go to church'; you *belonged* to the church. In fact, you and your Christian friends *were* the church.

So these three thousand brand new Christians in our reading from Acts were a church. As I said, they had no buildings and very little institutional structure (that was all being made up on the fly), but in the first few months of their life together they demonstrated all the major characteristics of a Christian community. Let me list them for you.

~

The Church is a Worshipping Community

Abraham Lincoln once said, 'If all the people who have ever fallen asleep in church were laid out end to end, they would be a great deal more comfortable.' There are many jokes like that, poking fun at boring services, long sermons, uncomfortable pews, and many other things. And yet, worship continues to be by far the most popular activity organized by most churches. Week by week, all around the world, hundreds of millions of Christians gather together to worship God.

We know this has been the case right from the beginning. Our reading from Acts says that the early Christians 'devoted themselves to...the prayers.' The definite article – '*the* prayers' – is in the original language, and it suggests that these were not private prayers but the formal prayers of a gathered community. The reading also says they 'spent much time together in the temple (and) broke bread at home.' 'The breaking of bread' was a common early Christian way of describing what we now call Holy Communion or the Eucharist, the meal of bread and wine that Jesus commanded his followers to share in remembrance of him. So, what the passage probably means is that the early Christians shared in the public prayers of the wider Jewish community in the Temple, but also met in homes to share the Lord's Supper with their fellow-disciples.

From the very beginning the church has been a community that gathers to worship God. Let's be clear again what worship is about. As I mentioned in a previous chapter, the physical setup of most churches today reminds modern people of a concert hall or theatre – settings in which the audience is largely passive, because they've come to be entertained. If the gathering makes them feel good, they will judge it to be a success.

The problem with bringing this attitude to a church gathering is that it shifts the focus away from God to ourselves. What am I getting out of this service? How is it making me feel? Excited? Bored? Annoyed? Joyful? Uncomfortable?

But worship isn't meant to be something the minister and the choir do to entertain the congregation. Worship is something the whole congregation offers to God. The pastor or minister isn't a soloist; they're more like a conductor, with the whole congregation as the orchestra. If there's an audience, it's an audience of one: God.

The most important act of Christian worship is the one Jesus himself left us: the Eucharist or Holy Communion. It's the only form of worship he specifically commanded us to offer, and in the early days it took the form of an extended family meal. This shows again the importance of coming *together* for worship; a family meal with only one person present is a contradiction in terms.

In Holy Communion we remember Jesus' death on the Cross and what it means for us, we give thanks for God's love, and we're nourished by the gift of the body and blood of Christ. More about this later in the chapter, where I will focus specifically on the Eucharist.

~

The Church is a Learning Community

In recent years there has been a huge emphasis on the importance of lifelong learning. For some this involves retraining for a new career; for others, there's a simple recognition of the fact that our world is constantly changing, and we need to work at keeping our knowledge and understanding up to date.

And yet many church members seem content to stop learning about their faith when they graduate from Sunday School—which, for some of us, is a very long time ago! This wasn't the case with the three thousand new followers of Jesus mentioned in our reading from Acts. 'They devoted themselves to the apostles' teaching.' What does that phrase mean?

Jesus had specifically commissioned the apostles—sometimes called 'the Twelve'—to pass on his teaching to the future generations of disciples. It's important to remember that this teaching was never meant to be purely academic. It's intended to have a practical impact. Jesus told the apostles to "Go therefore and make disciples of all nations, baptizing them in the name of the Father and of the Son and of the Holy Spirit and *teaching them to obey everything that I have commanded you*" (Matthew 28.19-20a, italics mine). The most important thing we need to learn is how to put the teaching and example of Jesus into practice in our daily lives.

At first, this learning would happen by word of mouth, as small communities gathered physically around one or more apostles and listened as they passed on the message of Jesus. But as the years went by, and as the church grew and spread, this became more difficult; the apostles couldn't be everywhere at once, and as time went by, they began to die (some of them because of persecution).

As we saw in the last chapter, the earliest written Christian documents were letters from apostles and other missionaries to churches they had founded, or to individuals within those churches. But as time went by, the recollections of the apostles of Jesus' life and teaching also began to be committed to writing. And so, almost certainly without anyone planning for it to happen, what we now call 'the New Testament' was written and collected. The New Testament contains the teaching of the apostles, just as the Hebrew scriptures or Old Testament contains the writings of the prophets and sages of ancient Israel.

So how do we, who can't actually listen to a living, breathing apostle, 'devote ourselves' to the apostles' teaching? The answer is, by reading and studying the Scriptures. As we read the Bible together, it's as if we're back in those early days when a group of believers would gather around Peter or Paul or John or Mary Magdalene, to hear again the message of Jesus. Whether we're studying in a small group, or listening to a sermon, we're taking our place in a learning community that has been doing its work for two thousand years.

However, I need to sound a note of caution here. Churches aren't called merely to repeat the same things from generation to generation. We have to take our specific context seriously.

Jesus' teaching was originally given in a Jewish context and in a largely rural environment. But when the apostles and missionaries began taking it out to the Gentile world, they had to apply it to different cultures and life situations—in large cities, where Judaism was only one of many religious systems on offer, and where they faced questions not addressed in the original words of Jesus. They had to identify the main themes of the message of Jesus, and then think about new questions in the light of those old themes.

The same goes for us today. Human nature may have changed very little in two thousand years, but the modern globalized consumer society we live in would have been unrecognizable to the early Christians. We have to think about that society in the light of the central principles of Jesus' message, and figure out what it means for us to be his faithful followers in this strange new world we live in. It's not just a matter of repeating Bible stories. Rather, as John R.W. Stott used to say, we need to build a bridge between the biblical text and the modern world – and that bridge needs to be firmly anchored at both ends.

~

The Church is a Loving and Caring Community

Or perhaps I should say, the church is *intended* to be a loving, caring community. Of course, the reality doesn't always match up to the ideal. I've been in churches where the members didn't even know each other's names, and newcomers, rather than being welcomed, were quickly frozen out. But that wasn't the case with the new church community born in Jerusalem on the Day of Pentecost. We're told that 'They devoted themselves to the apostles' teaching *and fellowship'* (Acts 2.42, italics mine). And this fellowship wasn't just an abstract ideal; it was lived out in costly and practical ways: 'All who believed were together and had all things in common; they would sell their possessions and distribute the proceeds to all, as any had need' (Acts 2.44).

The word 'fellowship' means having something in common, sharing together in something. The deeper the thing we have in common, the stronger will be the bond between us. For example, two of the longest standing relationships in my life were formed in my teens over a shared enjoyment of music. At the time, for my two friends and myself (as one of them expressed it) 'music was the meaning of life', and because we felt this so deeply, it created fertile ground for real fellowship between us. Of course, those friendships widened over the years to embrace many more areas of our lives, but music was the spark that got things going. Initially, it was the thing we had in common.

For Christians, our relationship with God through Jesus and our commitment to the way of Jesus is the deepest and most important part of our lives. When we find others who love and follow Jesus, we find an immediate bond with them; we can understand what makes them tick, and we can encourage each other in our journey of discipleship.

I was born in a working-class area of an industrial city in central England, but I spent my teenage years in a more middle-class rural area—mainly with my nose in a book! In later years, my ministry in the Anglican church has taken me into many different environments, where I've rubbed shoulders with people whose life experiences have been radically different from mine. These have included farmers in Saskatchewan, Dene and Inuit hunters in the high Arctic, and business and professional people in a large western city. On the surface, it would seem unlikely that I'd find common ground with these people, but over and over again, a shared commitment to the way of Jesus has been enough to bring us together.

But it's important to remember, as I said earlier, that according to our passage from Acts, fellowship isn't just about feelings.

A pastor friend of mine was meeting with some leaders from his comfortable suburban church. They were talking about the wonderful way in which fellowship was growing in their church, but my friend wasn't so sure. He said, "I think the test will be when the people who were planning on going on cruises this year buy their tickets as usual and then give them to the members of the church who can't afford to go on cruises!" That's the way it was with those early Christians in Acts: they shared their possessions with one another, and if any needed help, the others provided it.

~

The Church is an Outgoing Community

It's tragic when Christian churches are focussed inward and spend all their time thinking about their own buildings and programs, and their own survival. That wasn't what Jesus had in mind. Jesus wanted to change the world, and he planned to do it by sending out communities of disciples to spread his good news, invite others to become his followers, baptize them, and coach them in this new way of living. He wanted these new disciples to learn to make the world a better place by the way they lived. We can see this outreach going on at the end of our paragraph from Acts: 'And day by day the Lord added to their number those who were being saved' (Acts 2.47).

The book I've been quoting from is called 'Acts of the Apostles', and this title can sometimes give the mistaken impression that it was only the Apostles who were spreading the good news and leading others to faith in Christ. We get a bigger picture in Acts chapter eight. There we read about an outbreak of persecution against the disciple community in Jerusalem; many of the ordinary believers fled from the city and scattered to the country towns all around. Some of those who fled were leaders, but most would have been ordinary followers of Jesus. Given that they were running to escape persecution, you might have expected them to keep quiet about their commitment to Jesus in their new homes, so that they could stay out of trouble.

But in fact they did the opposite. 'Now those who were scattered went from place to place proclaiming the word' (Acts 8.4). Some of this 'proclaiming' might have taken the form of preaching in town squares and marketplaces and synagogues, but I think a lot of it was simply what an old friend of mine used to call 'gossiping the gospel.'

I can imagine a family of disciples of Jesus moving to a new community to escape from persecution. Maybe they started by staying with relatives while they were getting established in their new home. Eventually the breadwinner in the family would get a job or start a business; the family would make contacts, engage in conversation, and form new friendships. And in that context, opportunities would arise for them to talk about their faith in Jesus in a natural and friendly way. So, paradoxically, persecution of the church led to the growth of the church.

My friend Reed Fleming has a lovely way of describing this informal 'gossiping the gospel'; he calls it 'recommending Jesus'. I don't know about you, but I'm not shy about recommending things I've enjoyed, things that have enriched my life. My faith in Jesus is one of those things, so why would I be shy about recommending him to others? I don't have to be pushy and judgemental about it; I simply have to pray for guidance, and then be on the lookout for opportunities to share my faith (for me, they usually come in the context of trusting relationships).

The word that's sometimes used in church circles for this 'gossiping the gospel' is 'evangelism'. For some people this is a scary word; they associate it with high pressure tactics, disreputable activities of TV evangelists, and right-wing American politics.

Fair enough: if that word doesn't work for you, feel free not to use it. But it's quite clear that Jesus told his disciples to be 'witnesses' for him:

> "But you will receive power when the Holy Spirit has come upon you, and you will be my witnesses in Jerusalem, in all Judea and Samaria, and to the ends of the earth" (Acts 1.8)

In court, a witness is a person who tells their story, the things they have seen and experienced. So a Christian witness is a person who tells someone else about their experience of God, of Christian faith, of following Jesus, and the difference it's making in their daily lives. Witnesses don't have to argue and persuade; the Holy Spirit is actually quite good at that. The Spirit will take our words of witness and use them in the minds and hearts of those who hear them. In God's time, some of those people will decide they want to follow Jesus too. And so Jesus' plan for changing the world will go forward.

~

Joining the Family

This is where baptism comes in. Baptism is the pouring of water over people, or the immersion of people in water, in the name of the Father, the Son, and the Holy Spirit. Our passage from Acts tells us, 'So those who welcomed his message were baptized, and that day about three thousand persons were added' (Acts 2.41).

In one of the letters of the Apostle Paul, he tells us that the church is like a body, with Jesus as its head. 'Now you are the body of Christ,' he tells his hearers, 'and individually members of it' (1 Corinthians 12.27). Earlier in that chapter he spells out how his hearers became members of the Body of Christ:

> For in the one Spirit we were all baptized into one body—Jews or Greeks, slaves or free—and we were all made to drink of one Spirit (1 Corinthians 12.13).

So baptism is the act by which the Holy Spirit joins us to the Body of Christ.

In most churches, baptism is called a 'sacrament', a term that comes from a Latin word meaning 'promise'. Usually we make a promise with words, but in a sacrament, God makes a promise with both words and actions. An old definition of a sacrament is 'an outward and visible sign of an inward and spiritual grace' ('grace' here means 'gift'), 'given by Christ as a means and a pledge'.

What is meant by 'a means and a pledge'? A good example would be an engagement ring. One partner puts the ring on the other partner's hand; by this act they're becoming officially engaged, and it's also a promise, or pledge, of more to come: there's a wedding ahead! So by the act of baptism we're officially included in the Body of Christ, and there are many blessings ahead for us.

As we said, the outward sign in baptism is the pouring of water over a person, or the immersion of the person in the water, in the name of the Father, the Son and the Holy Spirit, as Jesus commanded. But what are the inward and spiritual gifts promised by this outward sign?

Baptism with water is a good symbol of the spiritual washing and cleansing we receive as our sins are forgiven by God. Baptism by total immersion (which is done today in churches of the Baptist tradition, among others) is a good symbol of going down into the grave with Jesus and then rising again to a new life with him. In some places in the Bible this beginning of a new life is described as being 'born again'. Baptism is also seen as the beginning of a life of discipleship, of following Jesus, and the gift of the Holy Spirit is promised to us to strengthen us in that new life.

Of course, we know that water by itself can't do these things; the person being baptized is also invited to put their faith (or trust) in Jesus. For those of us who were baptized as babies, as we grow up we learn to put our trust in Jesus and follow him.

~

The Family Meal

I called baptism a 'sacrament', which I defined as an outward and visible sign of an inward and spiritual gift from God. The other sacrament accepted by almost all Christians goes by several different names: the Lord's Supper, the Mass, the Eucharist, Holy Communion.

In one of his letters in the New Testament, Paul reminds us of how we got this sacrament in the first place:

> For I received from the Lord what I also handed on to you, that the Lord Jesus on the night when he was betrayed took a loaf of bread, and when he had given thanks, he broke it and said, 'This is my body that is for you. Do this in remembrance of me.' In the same way he took the cup also, after supper, saying, 'This cup is the new covenant in my blood. Do this, as often as you drink it, in remembrance of me.' For as often as you eat this bread and drink the cup, you proclaim the Lord's death until he comes. (1 Corinthians 11.23-26)

If baptism is the outward sign of becoming part of God's family, then the Eucharist or Holy Communion is our family meal. But it's not just a time to be jolly together! When we share this sacrament, we're actually casting our minds in five different directions. I sometimes refer to this as the five 'looks' of the Eucharist.

The first look is **the look backward**, in time, to Jesus' death on the cross. At the last supper Jesus told his disciples to 'do this in remembrance of me,' and in the passage I just quoted, Paul says, 'For as often as you eat this bread and drink the cup, you proclaim the Lord's death until he comes.' In the Eucharist we look back with gratitude to what Jesus did for us on the cross, promising forgiveness of sins to all who come to him. Because of the cross, we're assured that we can never be separated from the love of God. We look back in thanksgiving (the Greek word 'eucharist' means 'thanksgiving') and we celebrate these things, which is why in the Anglican church we say, 'We are going to *celebrate* the Eucharist together today.'

The second look is **the look upward** (yes, I know that heaven isn't really 'up there'; I'm using symbolic language here). One of the things Jesus said to his disciples at the last supper was "Apart from me you can do nothing" (John 15.5). Many of us have discovered the truth of this statement the hard way; we've attempted some task or project, but haven't asked for God's help with it, and we've fallen flat on our faces!

Jesus gives us his strength in many ways, but the Eucharist is one of the most important. As we receive this bread and wine with faith, our souls are nourished with the spiritual gifts of the body and blood of Christ. This isn't usually something we can detect with our emotions. You may not feel anything special when you receive the bread and wine, but don't let that bother you. It doesn't change the fact that Jesus has fed you with the bread of heaven.

In the broad spectrum of the Christian family, there have been different interpretations of Jesus' words 'this is my body' and 'this is my blood'. Some churches have taken these words very literally. Others have seen them as more symbolic (but remembering what we've already said about the tremendous power of a good symbol). Despite these disagreements, most Christians would agree that when we come to Christ's table and look up to him in faith, he quietly strengthens us to do the will of God in our daily lives.

If the first look is the look backward, and the second is the look upward, the third look is **the look around us.** The Eucharist isn't just something between me and God; it also involves my neighbours and connects me with believers all around the world. Listen to Paul:

> The cup of blessing that we bless, is it not a sharing in the blood of Christ? The bread that we break, is it not a sharing in the body of Christ? Because there is one bread,

> we who are many are one body, for we all partake of the one bread (1 Corinthians 10.16-17).

In other words, when we share the Eucharist, it not only strengthens our individual connection with Christ; it also brings us closer to each other. It's a family meal, a sign of the love between us as children of God.

Of course, it's vitally important that this be true in reality, not just in theory. Listen to Jesus:

> "So when you are offering your gift at the altar, if you remember that your brother or sister has something against you, leave your gift there before the altar and go; first be reconciled to your brother or sister, and then come and offer your gift" (Matthew 5.23-24).

Jesus is telling us that before we can worship God or offer him a gift, we need to do all in our power to get our relationships right. In many churches, this is recognised in a symbolic action that takes place in the Sunday service. Before people come forward to receive Holy Communion, they're invited to greet one another with a handshake or some other action, saying 'peace be with you,' or 'the peace of the Lord be with you.' This isn't meant to be just a sentimental act; it's an opportunity for us to be reconciled with our neighbours before we come to the Lord's table, as Jesus commanded us.

If the first look is the look backward, the second is the look upward, and the third look is the look around us, the fourth look is **the look forward,** to what is sometimes called 'the second coming' of Jesus. Listen to Paul again:

> For as often as you eat this bread and drink the cup, you proclaim the Lord's death *until he comes.* (1 Corinthians 11.26, italics mine)

The New Testament often pictures the kingdom of heaven as a feast. Sometimes it's even seen as a wedding banquet, with Jesus as the bridegroom and his church as the bride. It will be a great gathering of all the saints, including our own friends and relatives who have followed Christ and have gone before us.

We're promised that we'll see Jesus face to face, and we'll be together with him and with each other forever.

In the Eucharist we have a foretaste of this. It may only be a tiny piece of bread and a small sip of wine—it may be just a small gathering of followers of Jesus—but here already, we can get some sense of what the feast in the kingdom of God will be like. The life of heaven comes among us as we celebrate the Eucharist together; the strength and joy of heaven enter our lives in a new way.

The fifth and final look is **the look inward,** in self-examination. Listen to Paul again:

> Examine yourselves, and only then eat of the bread and drink of the cup. (1 Corinthians 11.28).

This verse reminds us that this isn't just an ordinary meal we're sharing together. This is a deep encounter with the risen Lord, so it's a good idea to prepare ourselves for it. The traditional Anglican *Book of Common Prayer* suggests three ways of doing this:

- *Repentance.* We look at our lives in the light of God's commandments, notice where we fall short, and resolve to make the necessary changes.
- *Faith.* We put our faith in Jesus again, trusting him to forgive our sins and give us daily strength to live in his way.
- *Love.* We ask ourselves where we're falling short of the love Jesus wants us to share with others. What changes do we need to make so we can walk the way of love more faithfully? Now's the time to make decisions about that, and to ask for the Holy Spirit's help.

One word of warning, though: there's no need for us to be nitpicky about this. Jesus isn't seriously expecting perfection from us; he knows us too well for that! Being a sinner doesn't disqualify you from receiving communion; if it did, none of us would be able to receive. What's asked of us is simply to turn from our sins and resolve to walk the way of Jesus; that's why we need to take this look inward.

These five 'looks' (backward, upward, around us, forward, and inward) tell us some of the most important meanings of the sacrament of the Eucharist or Holy Communion. In many Christian churches, including my own Anglican church, this is the central act of worship we offer to God week by week. This has been the mainstream tradition in Christianity right from the beginning, and today, more and more Christians are discovering the power of this family meal to draw us together into the presence of Jesus.

~

We Need the Church

Jesus never intended us to follow him alone; if we try to do that, we're doing something he never had in mind. Let me end this chapter with one more phrase in our reading from Acts: it says they 'devoted themselves' to these things.

'They devoted themselves...' In other words, they didn't say "We'll come together for worship on Sunday unless we have something better to do," or "We'll get together for our small group meeting unless the weather turns nice outside." No—they made these things their priority. And they knew it was worth it, because there's no better way to live the Christian life than the way Jesus planned it: together.

~

Sources

The description of the purposes of the church in Acts 2.42-47 is based on John Stott: *The Spirit, the Church, and the World: The Message of Acts* (Downers Grove; Inter-Varsity Press; 1990), 82-87.

I first came across the idea of the five 'looks' of the Eucharist in a book that has been out of print for many years: W.H. Griffith Thomas: *The Catholic Faith,* first published in 1904.

CHAPTER 8:

THE WAY OF LOVE

Back in the 1980s my young family and I lived in the community of Aklavik in the western Arctic, where I served as the minister at All Saints' Anglican Church. In the summer the community was accessible by air or by boat, but for several months each winter there was an ice road through the channels of the Mackenzie Delta across to Inuvik, a journey that normally took about two hours.

I didn't own a truck, but one weekend I borrowed one, and we drove over to Inuvik on Friday afternoon to do a little shopping and also to visit with our friends Ken and Aldene Snider (Ken was the minister at the Anglican church in Inuvik). We stayed over with them on Friday night, did our shopping on Saturday, and then began our journey home late on Saturday afternoon. All was going well, until about a third of the way over to Aklavik when the engine in the truck suddenly died. Closer inspection revealed a broken alternator belt, and I was not carrying a spare. The temperature that afternoon was about -30°C.

Fortunately a couple of other vehicles went by before long, and we were able to get rides home to Aklavik. When we got there, I immediately called Ken in Inuvik; he had a van and he was a good mechanic, and I asked if he could run out after church the next day and have a look at the truck. His response was immediate: "We'd better do it tonight, before the battery freezes."

So he got into his van, drove the two hours over to Aklavik and picked me up. We then drove back on the ice road, two thirds of the way to Inuvik, where the truck was sitting exactly where I had left it. Ken changed the alternator belt, boosted the truck, and let it run for a while to charge up the battery. He then followed me all the way back to Aklavik in his van to make sure I got there safely. When we got home I gave him a cup of tea, and he then set off back to Inuvik, getting home at about three-thirty in the morning. It was only a few short hours until he had to get up to lead his Sunday morning services.

Whenever I hear the biblical command to love your neighbour as you love yourself, I think of Ken Snider. What I saw that night (and it was typical of the man) was true love in action, expressed in service for a friend in need. His only thought was how he could help and bless another person. He was a true disciple of Jesus Christ.

~

Right at the centre of the ethical teaching of Jesus we find what we might call 'the way of love.' Everything else in the Christian life is built around this simple imperative to love God and love our neighbour.

Unfortunately, Christians haven't always realized this. In times past we tended to pay more attention to the Ten Commandments, the laws given by God to Moses in the Hebrew scriptures. There are two versions of them in the Bible, in Exodus 20.1-17 and Deuteronomy 5.1-21, and they are very similar to each other. God told the Israelites to have no other gods before the one true creator God. They were not to make idols for themselves, either of the gods of other nations or of their own God, because no idol or image can ever do justice to the glory and splendour of the one true God. They were not to make wrongful use of God's name, and they were to keep the Sabbath day holy by resting from all work. They were to honour father and mother, they were not to commit murder or adultery, not to steal or bear false witness against their neighbour, and not to covet anything that belonged to their neighbour.

These laws were given to Israel to guide their life as God's chosen people. There is nothing wrong with them, and obviously, if we all followed them, human societies would be much improved! But I find it interesting that when Jesus was asked which commandment in the law was the greatest or most important, he didn't quote any of the Ten Commandments. I've often wondered why that might be; could it be because love is not mentioned even once in the Ten Commandments?

~

Two Great Commandments

Here's Mark's version of the story of how Jesus identified the most important commandments in the Law of Moses.

> One of the scribes came near and heard them disputing with one another, and seeing that (Jesus) answered them well he asked him, "Which commandment is the first of all?" Jesus answered, "The first is, 'Hear, O Israel: the Lord our God, the Lord is one; you shall love the Lord your God with all your heart and with all your soul and with all your mind and with all your strength.' The second is this, 'You shall love your neighbor as yourself.' There is no other commandment greater than these." Then the scribe said to him, "You are right, Teacher; you have truly said that 'he is one, and besides him there is no other'; and 'to love him with all the heart and with all the understanding and with all the strength' and 'to love one's neighbor as oneself' – this is much more important than all whole burnt offerings and sacrifices." When Jesus saw that he answered wisely, he said to him, "You are not far from the kingdom of God." After that no one dared to ask him any question. (Mark 12.28-34).

"Which commandment in the Law is the greatest?" was a question Jesus probably expected to be asked at some point; it was 'in the air' at the time, and it's not hard to understand why. The Law of Moses (found in the first five books of the Bible) contains over six hundred separate commands; it's hard to *remember* them all, before you even start trying to obey them! Faced with that huge collection of laws, it's inevitable that people would choose a primary focus. Which commandments are central, and how could they be used to interpret the rest? This is what Jesus was doing when he identified the two greatest commandments: to love God with all your heart, and to love your neighbour as yourself.

It's often been pointed out that you can actually use Jesus' words here to summarize the Ten Commandments. The first four commandments are about how we love God with all our hearts: by worshipping only God, by not making idols, by respecting the name of God, and by keeping the Sabbath holy. The other six commandments are about how we love our neighbour as ourselves: we honour our parents, we respect life, we are faithful to our spouse, respect other people's property, tell the truth, and live a life of contentment.

But one important question to consider is what we actually mean by this word 'love'. Nowadays in English, we normally use it to describe an emotion, but that's not how people saw it in Bible times. As we said in a previous chapter, the New Testament was written in Greek, and C.S. Lewis once wrote a book called *The Four Loves* in which he explained the meaning of the four main Greek words for love. Let's look at them briefly.

The first word, *storge,* could probably be translated as 'affection'. Most characteristically, it's the affection of parents for their children, or children for their parents. But we could interpret it more widely as the love of familiar things or people. It's often associated with the word 'old' (in the sense of 'familiar'): 'my old man', 'this old guitar', and so on.

The second word, *phileo,* could roughly be translated as 'friendship'. Few people today think of friendship as a form of love, but in ancient times people certainly saw it in this way. My own personal belief is that one of the greatest blessings life has to offer is strong friendships.

Friendship often begins with a shared interest. My two longest-standing friendships were based on a common love of music; those relationships have since grown and expanded, but music was how they began. It's often been said that lovers look at each other, but friends look together at something else: a common interest.

The third word, *eros,* is where we get our modern word 'erotic'. We think of this in terms of sexual desire or romantic love, but in Greek the word is wider than that. It describes a form of love that is a response to something in the beloved, some form of beauty or goodness. Eros always includes the element of desire—to be with someone or something, to experience or possess them.

The fourth word is *agapé;* in the old King James Version it was usually translated as 'charity'. *Agapé* isn't about feelings; it's an action word ('serving' would probably be a good synonym for it). It's about volunteers serving in a soup kitchen or helping to build a Habitat for Humanity house. It's about people shovelling snow off the sidewalks of their elderly neighbours. It's about Ken seriously inconveniencing himself to rescue my truck on the ice road in the Mackenzie Delta. This kind of love is unconditional—you don't have to earn it or deserve it; it comes to you as a free gift. This is how God loves us, and this is how we're called to love one another. This is by far the most common word for love in the New Testament.

In Stephen Covey's book *The Seven Habits of Highly Effective People* he insists that love is a verb, not a noun. He illustrates this teaching with a story of a friend whose marriage was in trouble. "I don't love my wife anymore," he said. Stephen replied, "Then love her." The man was puzzled; "But you don't understand; the problem is that I don't love her anymore."

The difference between Stephen and his friend was that the friend was using the word 'love' to describe an *emotion,* while Stephen was using it to describe *actions*. It may be very difficult at times for us to decide to feel an emotion. However, it's always possible for us to make decisions about a course of action.

To understand this can be a very liberating thing. When I was a teenager, I worked as a paper boy. In those days in England, paper deliverers didn't work for a particular newspaper; they worked for a newsagent's shop and delivered all the newspapers for the area they were responsible for.

One morning when I went to the shop, I discovered there had been a terrorist bombing in London the night before, and the papers were full of the story (including photographs). My boss said to me, "I'm glad I'm not a Christian like you, because you

Christians are supposed to love everyone, and there's no way I could love people who would do anything like that."

At the time I didn't know how to answer him, but I do have an answer now. I totally agree that if the word 'love' is used to describe an emotion, it's very difficult to produce a good feeling toward people who commit atrocities. But Jesus' commandments aren't primarily about our feelings; they're about our actions. I love the way Paul describes this in one of his letters in the New Testament:

> Beloved, never avenge yourselves, but leave room for the wrath of God, for it is written, "Vengeance is mine; I will repay, says the Lord." Instead, "if your enemies are hungry, feed them; if they are thirsty, give them something to drink, for by doing this you will heap burning coals on their heads." Do not be overcome by evil, but overcome evil with good. (Romans 12.19-21)

I may not be able to produce a good feeling about my enemy, but I can give them a cup of coffee or a bowl of soup if they're in need.

Note carefully: to love someone in the sense of *agapé* doesn't always mean 'giving people what they want', or 'being nice to everyone.' In the case of parents and children, it's easy to understand that. There are times when good parents have no choice but to refuse requests from their kids, because they know it wouldn't be in the best interests of the kids to grant them. I once heard a well-known Anglican bishop say, "You're not loving people when you do for them what they can and should do for themselves." This is why we're told to love with all our *minds* as well as our hearts; sometimes we need to think hard about the best way to love people in a particular situation, and the answers aren't always easy to come by.

~

There's no escape from the command to love!

I'm sorry to have to break this to you, but the New Testament doesn't give us permission to hate anyone. Wherever you turn in the pages of the New Testament, there's no escape from the command to love. Let's take a few minutes to explore all the different people we're commanded to love.

~

First: love God

Jesus says, "You shall love the Lord your God with all your heart and with all your soul and with all your mind and with all your strength" (Mark 12.30). But it's important to realize that we offer this love to God in response to God's love for us, which always comes first. Listen to the words of the apostle John when he was an old man:

> In this is love, not that we loved God but that he loved us and sent his Son to be the atoning sacrifice for our sins...We love, because he first loved us. (1 John 4.10, 19).

Everything we have is a gift from God—not just the forgiveness of our sins, the unconditional love of God, and the right to think of ourselves as the children of God, but even the gift of life itself. All of this comes from God as a free gift. In response to this love, we love God in return by putting God first in our lives, by spending time with God in prayer and meditation, and also by following God's commandments. Jesus says, "If you love me, you will keep my commandments" (John 14.15).

I've been defining love in terms of action rather than emotion—and yet, we know the emotions are involved too. One of the great songs of praise in the Hebrew scriptures puts it like this:

> Shout for joy to the LORD, all the earth.
> Worship the LORD with gladness;
> come before him with joyful songs. (Psalm 100.1-2 NIV)

My experience is that the emotions tend to follow the actions—in other words, if I wait to *feel* love for others before I show it, I'll wait for a long time, but if I act in love first, I'm often surprised at how the feeling of love follows on. Likewise with God: as we act in obedience to God's will, so we often find our feeling of love and joy in God's presence begins to grow stronger.

It also needs to be said that part of loving God is *imitating* God. Jesus often told his disciples to be like 'your Father in heaven.' And that includes the way we love. The Bible shows us that God's love is *steadfast, unconditional, practical,* and *generous.* We're called to learn that same way of love.

~

Second: love yourself

Jesus says, "You shall love your neighbour as yourself" (Mark 12.31). Notice that he doesn't command us to love ourselves. He does something even more significant: *he assumes that we're already doing* it—that we can pattern our love for our neighbour on our experience of loving ourselves.

Sometimes people see self-love as a negative thing, and I get what they're saying. We've all met people who are totally full of themselves; they're selfish, self-centred, and conceited, putting themselves at the centre of the universe and ignoring the well-being of the people around them. Obviously, when Jesus commends self-love, that's not what he's talking about.

So what are some positive ways we can love ourselves? I can think of two. The first is what we might call *legitimate self-care.* This is really a very simple thing. When we're hungry, we find some food and we eat it. When we're cold, we reach for a fleece top or sweater, or turn up the thermostat. When we're lonely, we seek out friends and keep company with each other.

These are all good and necessary, and totally innocent. This is what Jesus means when he tells us to love our neighbour as we love ourselves. The good and proper care you give to yourself can be a model for the good and proper care you give to your neighbour.

There are times when we need to do this first, so we can be in good shape to help other people. In the airline industry, they refer to this as 'putting on your own oxygen mask first' before you try to help someone else with theirs. It's no help to your neighbour if you pass out from oxygen deprivation while you're trying to help them with their mask! It's much better to make sure you can stay conscious, and then you'll be able to help your neighbour stay conscious too! Many caregivers neglect this principle; over and over again, they put their own health aside and give all their time to caring for others. It sounds so good and loving, but in the end, there's a price to pay for it.

A second legitimate form of self-love is the *joyful acceptance of the person God has made us to be.* We're told in the Bible that God made human beings in God's own image. There are parts of this that we all share, but parts of it are unique to us as individuals – our own particular blend of physical features, gifts and talents, personality traits and experiences. These come to us as good gifts from our Creator. One of the songs in the Hebrew scriptures puts it like this:

> I praise you, for I am fearfully and wonderfully made.
> Wonderful are your works;
> that I know very well. (Psalm 139.14)

This song expresses the writer's joy at the unique way they had been put together by the loving hand of God. In our age of social media, there's an increasing tendency to feel compelled to fit into society's ideals and norms, and a corresponding increase in anxiety about our appearance and performance. The call to love ourselves comes as a healthy corrective to this, and a reminder to us to cultivate a sense of gratitude for all the good gifts the Creator has showered on us.

~

Third: Love your neighbour

It seems that Jesus discussed the two great commandments more than once. Luke tells a story of an expert in the Law standing up to test Jesus; he asked, "What must I do to receive eternal life?" Jesus replied with a question of his own: "What does the Law of Moses say? How do you read it?" The expert responded, "Love the Lord your God with all your heart and soul and mind and strength, and love your neighbour as yourself." "Well said," Jesus replied. "Do this and you will live."

But the expert wasn't done yet. "Yes," he asked Jesus, "but *who is my neighbour?"*

Jesus didn't give the man a direct answer to that question; he was not interested in giving the man permission to love some people and neglect others! Instead, in one of his most memorable stories, he defines how to be a good neighbour.

> "A Jewish man was traveling from Jerusalem down to Jericho, and he was attacked by bandits. They stripped him of his clothes, beat him up, and left him half dead beside the road.
>
> "By chance a priest came along. But when he saw the man lying there, he crossed to the other side of the road and passed him by. A Temple assistant walked over and looked at him lying there, but he also passed by on the other side.
>
> "Then a despised Samaritan came along, and when he saw the man, he felt compassion for him. Going over to him, the Samaritan soothed his wounds with olive oil and wine and bandaged them. Then he put the man on his own donkey and took him to an inn, where he took care of him. The next day he handed the innkeeper two silver coins, telling him, 'Take care of this man. If his bill runs higher than this, I'll pay you the next time I'm here.'
>
> "Now which of these three would you say was a neighbour to the man who was attacked by bandits?" Jesus asked.
>
> The man replied, "The one who showed him mercy."
>
> Then Jesus said, "Yes, now go and do the same." (Luke 10.30-37 NLT)

Note that in the time of Jesus, Jews and Samaritans didn't usually see each other as 'neighbours'; there were centuries of bad feeling between them. By identifying them in this way, Jesus teaches us that true neighbour love crosses barriers—whether between Christian and Muslim, gay and straight, left-wing or right-wing, indigenous people and settlers, rich and poor. If someone is in need, and I'm in a position to help them, then they're my neighbour, whether they look and speak and think like me or not.

Note also that the Samaritan never says, "This man is not my responsibility." The way Jesus tells the story, it seems there is no previous relationship between the two men, and yet the Samaritan still reaches out in love to the injured man and acts as a true neighbour to him.

In this masterful story, Jesus teaches us that true Christian discipleship is well within our grasp. The central issue of love for our neighbour simply means going through each day with our eyes wide open to the needs of those around us. We don't make excuses. If we're able to help them, we do so, without making a fuss about it. This sort of lifestyle is right at the heart of what it means to follow Jesus.

Fourth: Love your family

Throughout the Bible, family love is celebrated as a good thing. From the very earliest times marriage is commended as a gift of God in which two people become one flesh (you can read a symbolic account of this in Genesis 2.18-25). Children are seen as a gift of God; parents are encouraged to provide for them and guide them, and children are instructed to respect their parents and care for them in their old age. As we read about this subject, it's important for us to remember that for most people in Bible times, the basic family unit was not the nuclear family but the *extended* family, including grandparents and grandchildren, aunts and nephews and cousins and so on.

Of course, cultural norms around marriage and family have evolved and changed with time, even within the pages of the Bible. To give the most obvious example, the first two chapters of the Bible seem to assume a monogamous form of marriage, but in the rest of the Hebrew scriptures, polygamy is almost universal and is seen as a good thing (though its challenges are portrayed honestly too). This is not questioned until New Testament times, and then only very briefly.

Nowadays we would see things differently; today most Christians would see polygamy as misogynistic and would choose to focus on the very few places in the Bible where monogamy is described. Likewise, many modern Christians would want to question the teaching of some biblical authors about wives submitting to their husbands; how much is this a timeless truth, and how much is it a reflection on the cultures in which the biblical authors lived? Increasingly, also, there is an acceptance of gay and lesbian marriage as a legitimate development in the light of modern advances in our understanding of sexual orientation.

Through all these twists and changes, the heart of the idea of family has remained constant: the idea that love makes commitments and keeps them. This is the meaning of the Hebrew word *chesed,* which the *New Revised Standard Version* translates as 'steadfast love.' Biblical scholar John Goldingay, in his *First Testament* version of the Hebrew scriptures, translates it simply as 'commitment.' People in stable, loving families accept and embrace those commitments; they take responsibility for one another and provide security and mutual care.

~

Fifth: Love your fellow-believer

In New Testament times most people travelled from place to place on foot, on dusty or muddy roads, wearing open sandals on their feet. When evening came and they went indoors, you can imagine the state of their feet! In wealthy houses it was common to have a large stone water jar inside the door with servants ready to wash the feet of guests as they came in.

On the night before Jesus died, he and his friends shared a meal that we have come to call 'the Last Supper'; it was held in the home of a friend, in a room identified simply as 'the upper room.' In those days people didn't sit on upright chairs and eat at tables as we do. They reclined on couches around a low central table, angled in such a way that your neighbour's feet would have been in close proximity to your face!

For some reason, no foot washing had taken place that night. Were the servants not available for some reason? Were the disciples too proud to perform this menial task? We can't be sure. What we do know is that at a certain point, Jesus got up from the table, removed his outer garment, wrapped a towel around his waist, took a bowl of water and went around the group, washing the feet of each disciple.

The disciples were astonished when he did this; it was breaking all the social norms for the relationship between a master and his followers. Peter was indignant: "Lord, you will never wash my feet!" But Jesus was insistent. "Unless I wash you, you have no share with me" (John 13.8).

Listen to what Jesus said next:

> "Do you know what I have done to you? You call me Teacher and Lord, and you are right, for that is what I am. So if I, your Lord and Teacher, have washed your feet, you also ought to wash one another's feet. For I have set you an example, that you also should do as I have done to you. Very truly, I tell you, slaves are not greater than their master, nor are messengers greater than the one who sent them. If you know these things, you are blessed if you do them." (John 13.12b-17).

And a few verses later, he added,

> "I give you a new commandment, that you love one another. Just as I have loved you, you also should love one another. By this everyone will know that you are my disciples, if you have love for one another." (John 13.34-35)

Do you notice what Jesus is doing here? He's giving non-Christians the right to decide if we are truly his disciples, on the basis of whether or not they can see this kind of love among us. If they can't see it, then they have a right to judge that our claim to be his disciples is not true. Their judgement may be incorrect, but they have a right to make it, on the basis of the presence or absence of love.

I'm ashamed to say, many of us haven't lived up to that. Throughout our history (including today), we've often been better known for our quarrels than our love. We've even gone so far as to kill our fellow-Christians in wars, which must surely be the ultimate denial of Jesus' command to love.

So how should followers of Jesus practice this mutual love. Where should we start? I'd suggest a bare minimum starting point: members of churches could make the effort to learn each other's names! You may laugh at this, but I can say with all honesty that there are many Christians who have been going to the same church for decades but have never taken the trouble to ask each other their names. A next step could be to take the time to stay for the coffee hour after church; we could make a point of approaching people we don't know, introducing ourselves, asking them about themselves, and taking the time to listen and get to know one another. We can take the initiative in forming new friendships and be on the lookout for ways we can give or receive help. We might not be asked to wash each other's feet, but we could well offer to shovel each other's sidewalks!

~

Sixth: Love the poor and needy

The Hebrew scriptures are full of teaching about the obligation for God's people to help orphans and widows and stop trampling on the rights of the poor and needy. Two examples illustrate the way God wanted their society to be structured to care for the less fortunate.

First was the law of gleaning. When farmers were harvesting their fields, they were instructed not to take every single stalk of grain in the field. They were to leave some standing around the edges, so that the poor and needy could come afterwards and take some for themselves, so they would not starve. Likewise, the harvesters were instructed not to be too careful about picking up after themselves; if they dropped some stalks along the way they were to leave them for the poor.

Second was the Law of Jubilee. At the beginning of Israel's history as a people, the land was shared equally between their families. God was well aware that this equality would not continue; some would get richer at the expense of others. So God commanded that every fifty years there would be a reset button; every half century, the land was to return to the original owners. Human nature being what it is, there is no historical evidence that Israel actually every followed this law!

It's also interesting to note that care of the poor and needy was seen as the special responsibility of kings and governments.

Here's what one of those old Hebrew songs has to say on that subject:

> Give the king your justice, O God,
> and your righteousness to a king's son.
> May he judge your people with righteousness
> and your poor with justice.
> May the mountains yield prosperity for the people,
> and the hills, in righteousness.
> May he defend the cause of the poor of the people,
> give deliverance to the needy,
> and crush the oppressor...
> For he delivers the needy when they call,
> the poor and those who have no helper.
> He has pity on the weak and the needy
> and saves the lives of the needy.
> From oppression and violence he redeems their life,
> and precious is their blood in his sight.
> (Psalm 72.1-4, 12-14)

In the New Testament Jesus picks up on this theme. In his Sermon on the Mount (found in Matthew chapters 5-7) he identifies three duties of a godly disciple: prayer, fasting, and giving to the poor (in some versions of the Bible this is translated with the old English word 'almsgiving'). One of the commands regularly found on the lips of Jesus was "sell your possessions and give to the poor."

Toward the end of Matthew's gospel Jesus tells the story of the sheep and the goats. It's a last judgement scene; the nations are gathered before the Son of Man (the title Jesus used for himself), and he separates them into two groups like a shepherd separating the sheep from the goats. To one group he says, "Enter into God's kingdom, because when I was hungry or thirsty or naked or sick or in prison, you helped me." The people in this group are surprised. "Lord when did we do that?" The Son of Man replies, "When you did it to the least of these brothers and sisters of mine, you did it for me." But the other group are not so fortunate; they refused to help the poor and needy, and now they discover that in that moment of refusal, it was actually Jesus they were turning away.

It's safe to say, then, that followers of Jesus are called to be busy caring for those who are in need. In the modern world, we can often do this most effectively together. It's not just about individual followers of Jesus giving to charity; it's also about taking on new projects and making structural changes to our society. All too often, the way society is set up makes it difficult for the poor to get ahead – and, of course, race often plays a part in this as well. So the command to love the poor and needy asks us not only to give generously of our time and money, but also to change the way things are done in our communities, so that the world becomes a more just and compassionate place.

We've seen that we're called to love God, ourselves, our neighbour, our family, our fellow-believer, and the poor and needy. But there's one more person we're commanded to love.

~

Seventh: Love your enemy

Listen to Jesus:

> "You have heard that it was said, 'You shall love your neighbour and hate your enemy.' But I say to you: Love your enemies and pray for those who persecute you, so that you may be children of your Father in heaven, for he makes his sun rise on the evil and on the good and sends rain on the righteous and on the unrighteous. For if you love those who love you, what reward do you have? Do not even the tax collectors do the same? And if you greet only your brothers and sisters, what more are you doing than others? Do not even the gentiles do the same? Be perfect, therefore, as your heavenly Father is perfect." (Matthew 5.43-48)

Why are we called to love our enemies. Because that's how God acts. As Jesus notes, God doesn't withhold the sun and the rain from the wicked and undeserving; God showers blessings on them all, whether or not they love God.

This is the love that Jesus embodied when he died on the cross. As we saw in an earlier chapter, he refused to take vengeance on his enemies; he forgave them, and in doing so, he demonstrated the forgiving love of God. The story of the cross teaches us that God's love for enemies is right at the heart of the Gospel.

The early Christian teachers faithfully followed Jesus in encouraging this enemy-love. Listen to Paul in one of his letters:

> Do not repay anyone evil for evil, but take thought for what is noble in the sight of all. If it is possible, so far as it depends on you, live peaceably with all. Beloved, never avenge yourselves, but leave room for the wrath of God, for it is written, "Vengeance is mine; I will repay, says the Lord." Instead, "if your enemies are hungry, feed them; if they are thirsty, give them something to drink, for by doing this you will heap burning coals on their heads." Do not be overcome by evil, but overcome evil with good. (Romans 12.17-21)

You might be interested to know that in the first two or three centuries of Christianity, the vast majority of Christians were pacifists; it seemed very clear to them that the teaching of Jesus forbad Christians participating in war. Later, when the Roman empire became nominally Christian, theologians rethought this teaching and came up with various rules for deciding whether or not a particular conflict was a 'just war' that Christians could participate in.

The debate continues to this day, but whatever position we take on this subject, it's clear that love for enemies is commanded by Jesus, and hatred and vengeance are forbidden. Sadly, Christians have too often ignored this teaching and participated enthusiastically in the killing of others (including their fellow-Christians, which would have been inconceivable to the early disciples).

We often assume that this is impractical—and maybe it is. Maybe doing the right thing doesn't always 'work'. But take a moment to read this story that I found in a book called *A Culture of Peace*, by Alan and Eleanor Kreider and Paulus Widjaja:

A pastor in Indonesia saw an opportunity to do something risky. Through the local Association of Radio Broadcasting, he decided to approach the commander of a radical Muslim group, Hisbullah Shabillilah (the Soldiers of God), in the city where both the pastor and the commander lived. When the pastor first visited the headquarters of the Islamic group, he saw that on the walls were lots of swords and banners, with 'No Compromise!' written in big letters. But the pastor took time to befriend the commander of the soldiers and his followers, and to have dialogue with them about peacemaking.

On one of his visits he noticed that something symbolic had happened: the swords and banners had been taken off the walls. And the Muslim commander promised to send his members to attend the training on peacebuilding and conflict transformation that the pastor was organizing. Later on, in response to the December 26th 2004 tsunami disaster, the commander was eager to work together with the pastor and a local Centre for the Study and Promotion of Peace in a relief and trauma healing project in their area of Indonesia.

One day the commander told the pastor, "If only I had known you four years ago, I would not have had to lose fifty of my people who died in a war between Muslims and Christians. I used to think that spilling the blood of the Gentiles and the Chinese was permissible, but why is it different now? Is there something strange within me since I have learned to know you?"

~

Conclusion

Let's sum up what we've been learning in this chapter about the way of love.

Love reaches out from the heart of God to embrace us all, whether or not we deserve it. We don't have to earn it; it's the gift of God for every single human being, because God is a God of grace.

But this love isn't meant to stop with us. If it's real, it leads us to return God's love with all our heart and soul and mind and strength. And it doesn't stop there; it leads us out in love for ourselves, our neighbours, our families, our fellow-Christians, the poor and needy, and even our enemies. This is how God's kingdom spreads. This is how the world is transformed.

My good friend Daren Wride told me about a wonderful quote he heard from a well-known professor of preaching, Haddon Robinson. It went like this: 'Love is that thing which, if a church has it, it doesn't really need much else, and if it doesn't have it, whatever else it does have doesn't really matter very much.'

That's really it, isn't it? As Paul put it in another of his letters in the New Testament: 'And now faith, hope, and love remain, these three, and the greatest of these is love' (1 Corinthians 13.13).

~

Sources

The 'Love is a verb' exchange is found in Stephen R. Covey, *The Seven Habits of Highly Effective People* (Free Press; 1990).

The quotation about Muslim/Christian cooperation is from Alan and Eleanor Kreider and Paulus Widjaja, *A Culture of Peace* (Good Books; 2005), 126-127.

CHAPTER 9:

MONEY AND POSSESSIONS IN THE LIFE OF A CHRISTIAN

If you read the teachings of Jesus, one thing you'll notice is that he has a lot to say about money and its place in the life of a believer. Many people are surprised to discover that he said far more about money than almost any other subject, including sex! And he didn't just talk about giving; he was also interested in our overall attitude toward money and possessions, and the way they affect our lives.

This is why I'm dedicating a chapter in this little book to the subject of money and possessions in the life of a Christian. I've been asked several times if I'm making the subject out to be more important than it actually is, but I don't think so. It features highly in the teaching of Jesus, and in our modern world it's also a major competitor for God's place in our lives. We have to take it seriously.

~

Principles

As I read the Bible, I see three basic principles for thinking about the subject of money and possessions.

~

What's Ours is Really God's

> The earth is the Lord's and all that is in it,
> the world, and those who live in it,
> for he has founded it on the seas
> and established it on the rivers. (Psalm 24.1-2)

When you think about it, this seems pretty basic. If I make something on my own time, using materials I've grown or purchased, then what I make belongs to me unless I decide to sell it or give it away. God is the maker of the heavens and the earth; therefore they belong to God.

Rudy Wiebe's novel *The Temptations of Big Bear* takes place in the nineteenth century and begins with the negotiation (if you can call it that!) of Treaty Six between the Crown and the indigenous people of the northwestern Canadian prairies. One of the British officials is explaining to Big Bear (one of the Cree chiefs) the advantages of signing the treaty, one of them being that each family will receive a certain number of acres of land. Big Bear is mystified by this statement. "Who can receive land?" he asks. "From whom would he receive it?" It's clear that the idea that humans could be absolute owners of the land is quite foreign to Big Bear.

The Old Testament Hebrews would have understood this point of view. As we saw in the last chapter, the Law of Moses includes a provision that every fifty years all land was to revert to the family that originally owned it; also, all debts were to be forgiven and all slaves set free, so that inequalities in society would be erased and people would be free of poverty. Human nature being what it is, there's no evidence that anyone in Israel actually ever obeyed this law! But it's part of the Hebrew scriptures and it gives us God's point of view loud and clear. Only God is the absolute owner of anything. Everything we think we own, we're actually borrowing from him.

What does this mean for Christians as we think about our money? One implication, surely, is that we should stop thinking about 'giving our money to God.' The money already belongs to God, and we're responsible to God for how we use it—not only the portions we give away, but also the portions we keep for our own use. I once heard my dad say, "Instead of giving our money to God, we need to acknowledge that it all belongs to God and start asking him for an allowance!"

~

The Love of Money is Dangerous

In a forthright passage in one of his letters, the apostle Paul says,

> Of course, there is great gain in godliness combined with contentment, for we brought nothing into the world, so that we can take nothing out of it, but if we have food and clothing, we will be content with these. But those who want to be rich fall into temptation and are trapped by many senseless and harmful desires that plunge people into ruin and destruction. For the love of money is a root of all kinds of evil, and in their eagerness to be rich some have wandered away from the faith and pierced themselves with many pains. (1 Timothy 6.6-10)

Why do the biblical writers see the love of money as so dangerous? I think it's because they're keenly aware of its powerful potential as a false god.

Money and possessions claim to be able to give your life *meaning*, because if you can see you're getting wealthier, you feel your life has purpose and you're making progress toward your goal. They pretend to give you *security*; if you're wealthy, they say, you'll be able to handle any misfortune life sends your way. They promise *happiness and satisfaction*, on the understanding that the more possessions you have, the more you'll enjoy your life.

But these promises are lies. The only one who can give ultimate meaning, security, happiness, and satisfaction in life is God. Anything else that claims to be able to fill God's shoes is a false god, every bit as much as an idol made of wood or stone. If we see things in that light, it's clear that wealth is one of the leading false gods in the world today.

This was certainly the way Jesus saw it. The gospels tell of a time when he was asked to arbitrate a financial dispute between two brothers; he refused, but then he went on to talk about the dangers of greed. 'And he said to them, "Take care! Be on your guard against all kinds of greed, for one's life does not consist in the abundance of possessions" (Luke 12.15). Of course, in the modern world, there's a multi-billion-dollar advertising industry trying to persuade us that the abundance of possessions is *exactly* what your life consists of!

~

God Provides What is Needed

Toward the end of his life, when the apostle Paul was in prison in Rome, he often found himself in need. However, in one of the letters he wrote during that time he talks about how he has learned to trust God, not matter what the situation might be.

> I know the experience of being in need and of having more than enough; I have learned the secret to being content in any and every circumstance, whether full or hungry or whether having plenty or being poor. I can endure all these things through the power of the one who gives me strength. (Philippians 4.12-13 CEB)

The reason Paul was writing about this was that the Philippian Christians had sent him a financial gift to help him through his time of need. In their generosity, Paul sees the hand of God providing for him. And so he thanks them (apparently this wasn't the first time they'd helped him out in this way), and then he adds these words: 'My God will meet your every need out of his riches in the glory that is found in Christ Jesus' (Philippians 4.19 CEB). In other words, they had put God's purposes first by giving money to help Paul do God's work. In response, God would honour their generosity by providing for their needs as well. Jesus said much the same thing in the Sermon on the Mount: 'But seek first the kingdom of God and his righteousness, and all these things will be given to you as well' (Matthew 6.33).

But we do need to be careful here. God has promised to provide for our *needs*, not for our *wants*. All too often, my problem is that God and I aren't in agreement about what constitutes a valid 'need'! As a Canadian, I've gotten used to thinking of luxuries as necessities, but the biblical authors didn't make that mistake.

In the passage I quoted above from 1 Timothy, Paul says that if we have food and clothing, we should be content (I think if he had lived through a Canadian winter he might have added 'shelter' as well!). These necessities are what God has promised to provide for us. And of course, God also wants us to be part of the plan by which he provides for the millions who don't currently have food and clothing; taking part in that plan by our generosity is part of what it means to 'seek first the kingdom of God.'

At this point in my argument, a reasonable objection could be raised. "If God has promised this, how come so many millions around the world are living in poverty? Has Paul misinterpreted God's promises?" This is an excellent point, and I have two things to say in response.

First, in his letter to the Philippians Paul *isn't* writing to Christians living in destitution; his readers obviously had some disposable income, which they had decided to use to help him out. In response, he tells them he isn't the only beneficiary of their generosity; they, the givers, will be blessed by it as well. Most people in Canada today (though not all) would be in a similar situation to the Philippians: we may not think of ourselves as rich, but we do have some disposable income.

Second, when Paul *did* encounter Christians living in real destitution, his first response was not to tell them to trust God. Rather, he would turn to his wealthy friends and challenge them to give sacrificially to help their needy brothers and sisters. You can see an example of this in 2 Corinthians chapters 8 and 9.

~

Changes

I've spelled out three biblical principles for thinking about the subject of money and possessions. Now—if we take these principles seriously, what needs to change in our lives?

One of the gospel writers tells this story:

> (Jesus) entered Jericho and was passing through it. A man was there named Zacchaeus; he was a chief tax collector and was rich. He was trying to see who Jesus was, but on account of the crowd he could not, because he was short in stature. So he ran ahead and climbed a sycamore tree to see him, because he was going to pass that way. When Jesus came to the place, he looked up and said to him, "Zacchaeus, hurry and come down, for I must stay at your house today." So he hurried down and was happy to

> welcome him. All who saw it began to grumble and said, "He has gone to be the guest of one who is a sinner." Zacchaeus stood there and said to the Lord, "Look, half of my possessions, Lord, I will give to the poor, and if I have defrauded anyone of anything, I will pay back four times as much." Then Jesus said to him, "Today salvation has come to this house, because he, too, is a son of Abraham. For the Son of Man came to seek out and to save the lost." (Luke 19.1-10)

Do you see what happened in Zacchaeus' life? Until this point, he had lived by the values of the false god of wealth, which we might spell out as, 'It doesn't matter how you get it, just get as much as you can!' But when God's love touched Zacchaeus' life through his encounter with Jesus, he was transformed from a greedy to a generous person. That transformation wasn't complete when he stopped gouging the poor. It was only complete when he started giving to them instead.

We see the same idea in another place in the New Testament:

> Those who steal must give up stealing; rather, let them labour, doing good work with their own hands, so as to have something to share with the needy. (Ephesians 4.28)

You see the process? Instead of being a selfish person who steals from others, the thief needs to be transformed into a loving person who gives to others. This is what happened to Zacchaeus.

Do we earn the right to go to heaven by giving to the poor? Of course not. But being a Christian is about a lot more than going to heaven when we die. It's about learning to live the sort of life God planned for us, and discovering happiness and fulfilment in that life. Generosity is a vital part of what it means for us to learn to be like Jesus. And until we learn to be like Jesus, we won't find true contentment.

~

Needs

We need to learn to be generous with our time, our money, and our possessions. But who or what should we be generous to? The biblical writers suggest two directions for our giving.

~

Care for the poor and needy

This theme runs through the Bible from end to end. In Matthew chapter 25, Jesus tells us that when we feed the hungry, give drink to the thirsty, clothe the naked, and help others who are in need, we are actually helping him. The apostle Paul was also very concerned with the needy, and he spent a lot of time organising a collection for the relief of poverty-stricken believers in Jerusalem.

Today the needs are very great, and there are many avenues for generous giving. In my own Anglican Church of Canada, we have an aid organisation called the Primate's World Relief and Development Fund (see www.pwrdf.org), which supports projects run by partner agencies all over the world. There are many other excellent organisations: World Vision, the Canadian Foodgrains Bank, Mennonite Central Committee, Oxfam, and Rainbow Railroad are just a few that come to mind. There are also organisations that advocate for political and economic change, which is a vital part of improving the lives of the poor; two Canadian groups that come to mind immediately are Citizens for Public Justice and Kairos Canada.

All these organisations have a strong internet presence and it's easy to find out what they do and how they are structured. I would also highly recommend taking a look at a website called Charity Intelligence (www.charityintelligence.ca/), which is described as a 'trusted source for Canadian donors to get information about charities and intelligent giving.' Charity Intelligence has created profiles on over 800 Canadian charities, assessing their transparency and accountability, their need for funding, their cost efficiency, and, where possible, their social impact.

~

Supporting the work of the church

The earliest Christians had no church buildings, and there was also great variety in the way that pastors and Christian workers were supported. To use the apostle Paul as an example, sometimes he supported himself by working in his trade as a tentmaker, while at other times he was supported by the gifts of others and so was able to work full-time as a missionary and church-planter. But his instruction on the subject is very clear: 'In the same way, the Lord commanded that those who proclaim the gospel should get their living from the gospel' (1 Corinthians 9.14).

If the work of the church is going to continue, it needs to be financed. Staff need to be paid, buildings need to be cared for, and programs need to be supported. The need is always there.

And this isn't just about our own local church; the whole church is a family, and in that family, those who have much can help those who have little. When I was a pastor in small rural parishes, I was very grateful that in our Anglican Church of Canada, money sent to our national office from richer areas of Canada could be used to help finance ministry in isolated northern churches like ours. Without that help, the churches I served could not have survived. It's always tempting for us to think only of our local needs, but this should be resisted. 'Charity begins at home' is not a principle you can find anywhere in the teaching of Jesus!

~

Steps

A friend of mine tells the story of how, when he first became a churchgoer in his forties, he was very alarmed when his wife put a two-dollar bill on the collection plate; he thought that was way too generous! Later, after he'd been a member of the church for a while, he had a better understanding of the needs of the congregation and how it was financed, and his giving became more generous and more realistic. Eventually, as he read the Bible, he adopted the practice of proportional giving: choosing a percentage of his income and giving it away (in his case, it was ten percent, which in the Hebrew scriptures is called a 'tithe').

How much should we give? We can't be legalistic about this. Jesus never mentions the tithe and it's not commanded anywhere else in the New Testament, but before we heave a sigh of relief and close our wallets, we should remember that when Jesus changed the laws in the Hebrew scriptures, he usually made them *more* stringent, not less! The righteousness of his followers was to *exceed* that of the scribes and Pharisees. They were to avoid not only murder but also anger, and they were to love not only their friends but also their enemies (see Matthew 5.21-48). The Pharisees were well-known for their strict tithing; what might it mean for us to exceed that level of righteousness?

Sometimes dollar amounts can be misleading. The gospels tell a story of Jesus sitting in the Jerusalem Temple with his disciples, not far from where the huge collection boxes were placed. Many religious people were coming up and making a big show of tossing valuable coins into the boxes. But then, as Jesus watched, a poor widow came quietly up to the boxes and put in two small copper coins: a paltry sum, you might think. But Jesus would disagree:

> "Truly I tell you, this poor widow has put in more than all of them, for all of them have contributed out of their abundance, but she out of her poverty has put in all she had to live on." (Luke 21.3-4)

Maybe his message was that the amount we give isn't as significant to God as the amount we have left after we give!

My observation is that most Christians go through three steps as they grow in their understanding of Christian generosity.

~

Casual giving (also known as 'Jesus-tipping'!)

This is where my friend started when his wife put two dollars in the collection plate. Let's be frank about this: when we start out in the Christian life, our giving is more like the tipping some of us do in restaurants. If the service is good, we might leave a more generous tip, but it doesn't amount to very much.

~

Responsible giving

Gradually, as we get involved in a local church, we get a better understanding of its finances, its level of income, and the expenses involved in running the place. Maybe we look at the annual budget, and then we take a look around the congregation on a Sunday, count heads, do the math, and come to some idea of what a reasonable share for us might be. I'm told that in some churches this is how they handle their annual budget: they figure out how much they need for the year, and then mail out notices of what each member's share is going to be (I think there'd be a mass exodus from my parish if I tried anything like that!).

I call this 'responsible giving,' because I'm trying to do my bit as a responsible member of my church. It's a big improvement on Jesus-tipping, but it has one shortcoming: it's based on *the church's need to receive,* rather than on *my need to give* so that I can grow into a more loving and more generous person.

~

Proportional Giving

This third step has nothing to do with the needs of the organisation; it's based on my level of income. You simply look at your annual income, choose a percentage to give away, and then build your budget around that.

You might think a person would need to be very well-off to do that, but in my experience that's not the case. Some of the most faithful proportional givers I know are actually quite poor, but they continue to be generous. Years ago, one of them said to me, "God's promise to look after us is worth far more than half a million in the bank!" She was a person who was learning to live her whole life on the basis of trust in God. She was also one of the most generous people I have ever known in other areas of her life.

How should we choose our level of giving? Only you can decide that. But I do need to sound a warning about one thing I hear from time to time. Sometimes people say, "Right now my income is low and my expenses are high, so I can't give too much. Once things are under control, I'll be able to give a lot more."

In my experience, that rarely comes about. What tends to happen is that as our income increases, our lifestyle expands to match it, so we still don't have enough. We need two cars, and a bigger house, and a newer computer, and we can always find excellent reasons why these are *needs*, not luxuries.

If I wait until I'm richer before I start giving sacrificially, I'll probably never start. What will actually happen is that the false god of wealth will wrap its chains more and more securely around my heart. If I don't give generously while I'm poor (remembering the poor widow as we define 'generous), I probably won't give generously when I'm rich either.

Jesus says, "Whoever is faithful in a very little is faithful also in much" (Luke 16.10). The time to learn Christian generosity is almost always now. If I consider myself poor, I can rejoice to be able to learn the joy of Christian giving before the love of money has me hooked. If I'm rich (and on a global scale, almost all western Christians are rich), then I need to get started right away before money chains my heart to the earth even more securely. It's rarely a question of what I can afford. Far more often, it's a question of who or what comes first in my heart.

I'd like to share a word of testimony about this—not in order to boast, but hopefully to give you some encouragement.

I first heard about tithing when I was new to Christianity. I was a teenager at the time, and my only income was from my paper route, which paid me the princely sum of £1 a week (UK money). So I decided to give ten percent—ten pence—to my church, and that's what I did.

Once I started, I never gave up. In 1978 when I was a young evangelist, I was making about four hundred dollars a month, so my tithe was forty dollars a month for my church. As the years went by, I began to expand my definition of a tithe: not just money given to the church, but also to the poor and needy. I got involved with fundraising efforts for Habitat for Humanity and World Vision. In our family we've taken on sponsor children in the developing world, and also committed to the ongoing support of a friend's inner city street ministry. And so it goes on.

What I've discovered is that the more I do this, the more I enjoy it. There are two things I've learned.

First, ***you don't need a lot of possessions to be happy***. My wife and I live in a very small townhouse, with one (moderate) income, and we drive small, fuel-efficient cars. It's not that we don't have nice things: we have a piano, two very good guitars, and a truckload of books, and we make regular trips overseas to visit family in England and Wales. But we always try to keep Jesus' words in mind: "Do not store up for yourselves treasures on earth...for where your treasure is, there your heart will be also" (Matthew 6.19, 21). And I think we would both say that we live a very happy and contented life.

The second thing I've learned is that ***the greatest joy in life is generosity***. If you're addicted to acquisition, you'll never be content and you'll never have enough. But generosity can be a positive addiction; the more you give, the more you love to give—not just money, but also time and talents—and the more you share in the joy of Jesus, whose whole life was a gift offered to God and others. 'For you know the generous act of our Lord Jesus Christ, that though he was rich, yet for your sakes he became poor, so that by his poverty you might become rich' (2 Corinthians 8.9).

~

I want to close this chapter by quoting one more thing Paul said about this subject: 'God loves a cheerful giver' (2 Corinthians 9.7). If I give enormous amounts of money to the poor, but do so grudgingly, out of a sense of obligation, I still haven't let the gospel do its liberating work in me. I'm still refusing to let the Holy Spirit change me from a hoarder into a giver.

You sometimes hear the slogan, 'Give until it hurts.' That doesn't go far enough. I don't want to stop when it hurts; I want to keep going until it feels good! I want to let the Holy Spirit transform me until I reach the point where love and generosity are the most important and joyful parts of my life—the point where the giving of money is just an outward sign of the giving of my whole life in service to God and others.

Many years ago I knew a man called Marvin, who started a Christian bookstore in a small town in northeastern Saskatchewan. I passed through that town three times a week, on my way between the various communities where I served Anglican churches, so I got to know Marvin quite well. He was years ahead of Chapters and their built-in coffee shops: he always had a pot of coffee and a stack of old-fashioned Styrofoam cups on hand, and he encouraged his customers to stop and visit with him.

Marvin was a Mennonite, and I was an Anglican minister, and we got to be good friends. Before long, Marvin was giving me books and refusing to let me pay for them. One day I said to him, "Marvin, you are never going to make any money if you keep giving books away like this." He laughed; "Yeah," he said, "but I'm having a lot of fun doing it!" A year or two later, when I suddenly found myself without a car for a couple of months, he immediately lent me one of his vehicles and refused to take a cent from me for it.

I lost touch with Marvin years ago, but I have never forgotten him. He taught me a lot about Christian generosity—not by his words, but by his actions. I often pray for the grace to be like him.

~

Sources

The story about Big Bear is taken from Rudy Wiebe's novel *The Temptations of Big Bear* (Toronto; McClelland and Stewart; 1973).

CHAPTER 10:
MAKING A DIFFERENCE

I was once asked to preach at an ordination service of two new priests. I began my sermon that night with these words:

> Tonight we're gathered here in this cathedral to celebrate with our new priests as they step *back* from front line Christian ministry and take up the secondary role of ordained pastors in the church of Jesus Christ.

It might have been my over-active imagination, but at that point I'm pretty sure I heard a few gasps from the congregation!

I wasn't joking, and I wasn't trying to be provocative. I really believe that, in the context of the total ministry of the church of Jesus Christ, the role of ordained clergy is secondary. The front-line ministry of the church happens seven days a week in the lives of ordinary Christians.

It happens in a home, as the members of the family learn to set selfishness aside and serve one another in the name of Christ. It happens in an office, as a Christian businessperson struggles with the question of what it means to follow Jesus in an atmosphere dedicated to the creation of wealth. It happens in a convenience store as a Christian serving behind the counter does his best to treat his customers as human beings loved by God. In happens in a court of law, when a Christian lawyer asks herself the question, "If Jesus was in my shoes today, what would he do?" It happens every day, as followers of Jesus learn to love their enemies, pray for those who hate them, care for the poor and the suffering, and share the good news of Jesus with others.

This is where we need to start when we're thinking about the ministries to which God is calling us as Christians. Ministry isn't just about what we do in church on Sundays or how we keep the organisation of the church going. Ministry is about what God is doing out in the world on a daily basis. The God we read about in the Bible is passionately committed to the transformation of the world.

And this has implications for me, as a Christian pastor. It means that success isn't primarily about having a full church on Sundays (or whenever our church happens to meet). No—success is when the members of our church go to work on Mondays, seeing themselves as disciples of Jesus and partners in God's mission to change the world for good. It's when they go to work, not just to make a *living*, but to make a *difference* in the world for the kingdom of God. Of course, this also applies to those who go to school, and those who are unemployed, and those whose primary work is to make their homes places of love and nurture. Wherever they go, Christians are called to be ministers of Jesus Christ. As Paul says in one of his letters, 'And whatever you do, in word or deed, do everything in the name of the Lord Jesus, giving thanks to God the Father through him' (Colossians 3.17).

So Christian ministry is not primarily something done by people wearing clergy collars in church buildings. It's the work of the entire Christian community serving God in the world. No one is left out. Every member of the team is important, and every member has gifts from God that are necessary to the whole team.

~

A Team with a *Vision*

In the seventeenth century a great fire burned down a huge part of the city of London, including many churches. Sir Christopher Wren was a great architect who designed many of the new churches and other buildings after the fire, including the present St. Paul's Cathedral with its distinctive dome. The story is told of a team of visitors walking around the construction site of the new cathedral. They knew very little about building, so they kept stopping and asking various workers what they were doing. One man replied, "I'm digging a hole, can't you see?" Another one said, "I'm hauling stones, obviously." But a third looked at them with a smile and said proudly, "I'm helping Sir Christopher Wren build a great cathedral."

That man had a sense of vision, and because he saw the big picture, he understood how important his little job was. In the same way, we disciples of Jesus can see ourselves as members of the construction team of the great Architect of the Universe, helping to rebuild a ruined world according to God's great design. In this project, what we need most of all is a sense of how our work fits into the whole plan.

What is that plan? In the Lord's Prayer we pray, "Your kingdom come, your will be done, on earth as in heaven." This is parallelism, a form of Hebrew poetry in which the second line repeats the first, only in a slightly different way. So if we ask, "What does it mean for God's kingdom to come?" the reply is "It means that God's will is done on earth as it is in heaven." At the moment, of course, this is not the case; the reason there is so much suffering and misery in the world is that God's will is *not* being done on earth as in heaven. But as God's kingdom advances in the world, as God's loving will is done, then our broken world will be healed. This is what we're all about as Christians: living to heal the world and restore it to God's original dream.

What is ministry? Ministry is simply using your God-given gifts and talents to help God's plan for the world become a reality. A few years ago when I was at summer school in Regent College in Vancouver, one of the courses being taught was called 'A Spirituality of Ordinary Life.' Unfortunately I wasn't taking that class, but it was meeting each day in the same classroom as my course, only at a different time. Because their teacher never cleaned his chalkboard, we often got to read interesting little snippets from his class. One day when we came in, there was a chart on the chalkboard. Along the top, at the head of each column, was a list of various roles God plays in the world—God as teacher, God as provider, God as healer, God as protector, and so on. Then under each role was a list of human occupations corresponding to that role. For instance, under 'God as Teacher' were teachers, pastors, university professors, parents, and so on.

Under 'God as Provider' were farmers, grocers, grocery truck drivers, and other relevant occupations.

The message of this chart was that every legitimate human occupation is a way of fulfilling God's plan. A teacher who devotes himself to the shaping of young minds, a scientist who expands our knowledge of diseases and their possible cures, a police officer who devotes herself to the protection of the vulnerable—these people are fulfilling God's plan every bit as much as the pastor leading a church service on Sunday morning.

This means that followers of Jesus can't build firewalls to keep God out of their work. Jesus is Lord at your place of work as well as at church. Sometimes this means wrestling with hard issues. What does it mean for a Christian police officer to carry a gun and be trained to use it? What does it mean for a Christian in business to be part of a corporation that utilises cheaper labour overseas? These are tough questions with very few easy answers, but wrestling with them is part of our responsibility as Christians committed to following Jesus as Lord at work as well as at church.

So this is the vision: God wants to heal the world, and the job of the church is to help that happen. That means we go out into the world to share the love of God in both words and actions. In words, we share the Good News of Jesus and invite people to become his followers. In actions, we do all we can to alleviate suffering and make the world the kind of place God wants it to be. Keep this vision in mind as we continue to talk about Christian ministry.

~

A Team with *No Passengers*

Imagine the Saskatchewan Roughriders are coming to Edmonton to play against the Elks. The game starts; the Roughriders move out onto the gridiron and take their places. Then, to everyone's amazement, out to face them on the other side comes the Edmonton Elks' *coach*—alone! And when they're challenged about this unusual strategy, their response is simple: "He's better than any of the players, so why shouldn't he do it?"

If the Elks field their coach as the sole player in every game, two things are going to happen. First, the coach is going to get wiped out. Second, the players are going to lose their skills, because they don't have opportunities to use them. This situation is bad not only for the coach; it's bad for the team as well.

In many churches the people think the coach should do all the ministry. They think they haven't really been prayed for unless the priest prays for them. They haven't really been visited unless the pastor visits them. They haven't really been loved unless the pastor loves them. They haven't really been taught unless the priest teaches them. What's the result of all this? The pastor gets wiped out, and the church members don't grow in their ability to use the gifts God has given them.

The reason we have this problem is that we've inherited a faulty model of church life. I've been using the model of a team and its coach, but many church members are working with an entirely different model: **a bus and its driver.** In this model, the pastor is the bus driver, and the congregation are the passengers. And this is why they get so annoyed when the pastor suggests that they ought to do some of the ministry in the congregation. It's as if they'd paid for their bus ticket, only to discover an hour into the trip that they were expected to do some of the driving themselves. "Why are you expecting *me* to drive?" they ask. "That's what I pay *you* to do."

These people need to see that this model of a bus and its driver is completely unbiblical—and that's not just because there were no buses in New Testament times. Every image of the church used in the New Testament stresses the team concept. The Apostle Paul says the church is like a body with many parts, and he points out that every part has a vital role to play if the body is going to be healthy.

So the proper model for church life is **a team with a coach**. The purpose of the church is to help Christians grow so they can do God's work in the world. The role of pastors is to train and mentor Christians for that work. Paul says,

> It was he who "gave gifts to people"; he appointed some to be apostles, others to be prophets, others to be evangelists, others to be pastors and teachers. He did this to prepare all God's people for the work of Christian service, in order to build up the body of Christ. (Ephesians 4.11-12 GNT)

The church is not a bus. Healthy churches don't carry a lot of passengers. They may sometimes carry injured players who need time to rest and heal from their wounds. They may also carry retired players who have spent most of their energy in the past, and now mainly do the work of praying for the more active members of the team. But these are exceptions to the general rule. In most cases, as soon as they are well again, injured players will be redeployed on God's team so that God's work in the world will go forward.

~

A Team with *God's Gifts*

Pastors sometimes use intimidating language when they talk about spiritual gifts. They talk about people having the gift of 'discernment,' or the gift of 'miracles,' or (scariest of all, to some people) the gift of 'speaking in tongues.' I found it refreshing a while back to hear someone say of a university chaplain that he had 'the spiritual gift of hanging out' with students. God had given him the ability to go where students went, do things with them, and strike up significant conversations.

In the lists of spiritual gifts in the Bible, there's often this combination of natural and supernatural abilities. The supernatural gifts tend to get our attention, but the natural abilities are just as important. For instance, one of the characters in the book of Acts is named Joseph, but the apostles gave him a new name, Barnabas, which means, 'Son of Encouragement.' I can imagine the discussion after church one day in Antioch. "That Joseph! No matter how bad you're feeling, all you need to do is talk to him, and he can lift you up." Or the two young preachers comparing notes about their experiences, and one of them saying, "I thought I'd made a real mess of that sermon, but old Joseph came over and pointed out two or three things he really liked about it, and I felt so much better." Joseph had the gift of encouraging people; that's why they nicknamed him Barnabas.

Look at Romans 12.3-8:

> Because of the grace that God gave me, I can say to each one of you: don't think of yourself more highly than you ought to think. Instead, be reasonable since God has measured out a portion of faith to each one of you. We have many parts in one body, but the parts don't all have the same function. In the same way, though there are many of us, we are one body in Christ, and individually we belong to each other. We have different gifts that are consistent with God's grace that has been given to us. If your gift is prophecy, you should prophesy in proportion to your faith. If your gift is service, devote yourself to serving. If your gift is teaching, devote yourself to teaching. If your gift is encouragement, devote yourself to encouraging. The one giving should do it with no strings attached. The leader should lead with passion. The one showing mercy should be cheerful. (CEB)

This list has the same combination of the unusual and the ordinary. Some people have the gift of prophecy – that is, they're able to hear God speaking to them with a message to pass on to others. Maybe that seems like a pretty high-calibre gift and not one an ordinary Christian like you or me could aspire to. But then at the end of the list, we see the gift of compassion. Some people seem to have the ability to feel the pain of other people and reach out to them in love.

Think about all the gifts the Christian church needs in order to fulfil its mission for God. We need parents with the skills to bring up children in an atmosphere of love and nurture so they can grow into mature disciples of Jesus. We need people with MBAs who can think through the ethical issues of being in business today and run their companies in such a way that God's will is done on earth as in heaven. We need teachers who understand that all truth is God's truth and that the forming of young minds is a sacred trust from God. We need politicians, judges, and lawyers who will put doing the will of God ahead of narrower concerns in their work. And in the daily life of a congregation we need musicians who can lead us in worship, people with financial skills to handle our books, and administrators to make sure everything is run efficiently. We need compassionate people who will give their time to listening and being there for others who are in pain, and gifted evangelists who will share the good news with non-Christians and help them decide to become followers of Jesus. We need people with skill in maintenance to look after our buildings, and good teachers for our Sunday Schools and adult study programs. And I haven't even begun to talk about the ministry of pastors yet!

There is hardly a human skill in the world that God does not need for the extension of his kingdom. Or, to look at it the other way around, if God asks us to do a job, you can be sure he will give us the gifts we need in order to complete it.

~

A Team with a *Plan*

In Mark 1.29-39 we see Jesus doing three things.

First, we see him **meeting human needs.** He heals Simon's mother-in-law from a high fever. Later that day many sick people are brought to him, and he heals them all. This seems familiar to us, because it follows the pattern of much of the ministry of Jesus: when he sees human suffering, he alleviates it by the power of God.

Second, we see him **spreading the message of the kingdom of God.** Mark says, 'he went throughout all Galilee, proclaiming the message in their synagogues...' (Mark 1.39). We're familiar with this role of Jesus, too: the teacher and preacher, the one who announces God's message and invites people to respond to it.

Third, we see him **in prayer.** Mark says, 'Early in the morning, well before sunrise, Jesus rose and went to a deserted place where he could be alone in prayer' (Mark 1.35 CEB). In his time of prayer, Jesus obviously listened for God's guidance, because later on he was able to say 'no' to the expectations of his disciples and move on to the next thing he believed God had in mind for him.

These three things are the blueprint for the way we Christians make a difference in the world. This passage calls us to make a difference by our actions, our words, and our prayers.

Making a difference by our actions might start out with being more intentional about ethical behaviour in our workplace. I once had the privilege of listening to a Christian businessman talking about this. He was a commercial realtor, and he talked about the constant pressure to do business in a way that was less than ethical, a way that took moral shortcuts. He was quite candid about how much money a person could make if they were willing to go along with this, but he was also aware that this was not what he was called to as a Christian. He was called to take the higher ground and do business honestly and ethically. As I listened to him speaking, I felt my excitement rising. It was clear to me that this man had made a difference to the moral climate of the business community in our city. Edmonton was a better place to do business because of him. This is what Christian faithfulness looks like.

Often, of course, it will go further than that. I know followers of Jesus who help out regularly with programs run by inner-city churches or parachurch organisations, serving meals and helping with education programs for those suffering from poverty or homelessness. Others are involved with Habitat for Humanity, helping provide affordable housing for people who would otherwise not be able to enjoy it. Others are involved in political action, calling our leaders to account for their decisions in the spirit of the Old Testament prophets who challenged their kings to follow God's laws and treat the vulnerable with love and care.

Making a difference by our words involves sharing the good news of Jesus Christ with others. This doesn't mean we all have to become preachers or evangelists. The New Testament uses a different word to describe this work we do; it calls us 'witnesses.' Witnesses in a court of law don't have to argue the case; that's the job of the lawyers. All the witnesses have to do is tell the truth about what they've experienced.

If you've responded to the invitation to become a follower of Jesus, you've probably already begun to experience God at work in your life. God doesn't want you to keep that story to yourself. Your story can help reach other people as well.

Some years ago, when I was serving in a previous parish, a man I'll call Larry (not his real name) showed up one Sunday at our church. I'd never seen him there before, but it turned out that he was going through a difficult patch in his life, and a member of our congregation who was a close friend of his had invited him to church. Over the next few months, Larry gradually got involved in the life of our parish, and his personal faith grew to the point that he wanted to commit his life to Christ in baptism. Eventually he was baptized, and he continues to be a faithful and growing Christian today.

Not too long after Larry's baptism I was teaching a course about evangelism at our church. One of the participants was the friend who had first invited Larry to church; I'll call him Jack. One evening we were talking about sharing our faith stories with people who weren't believers. Most of the people in the group found this a rather scary idea, but then Jack spoke up. "You know, I did share my story with someone else once," he said. "I shared it with Larry. And now he's a Christian."

There were many links in the chain that led Larry to faith in Jesus, but one of the first of them was the day his trusted friend had the courage to tell him the story of Christ's work in his life. This wasn't a matter of Jack asking, "Are you saved?" or giving him a tract or a canned gospel presentation. It was a conversation that took place in the context of a long-standing friendship, in which one friend shared with the other the best thing he had to offer: his relationship with God. And that made all the difference.

Our actions and our words are part of God's plan to heal the world. However, we mustn't forget the third part of the plan: **making a difference by our prayers.**

My wife, Marci, wasn't always a member of the Anglican church. In her early teens she shopped around a bit and tried a few other churches. What drew her back to the Anglican church was the strength of its prayers for the whole world. She didn't enjoy the prayers of churches that only asked God's help for their own members and the problems they were facing and forgot to pray for those dying of starvation in the majority world, or to ask God's wisdom for our political leaders. Not that God doesn't care about Aunt Lucy's cancer surgery, but God wants our prayers to be far-reaching, touching not only the people we know and love, but all the people around the world who are known and loved by God.

You and I can't heal the world. Only God has the power to do that. Our words and actions are part of God's plan, but without God's help they're still inadequate. Jesus knew this; that was why he built regular prayer into his life. Luke tells us that it was Jesus' habit to 'withdraw to deserted places and pray' (Luke 5.16). In this way, he aligned his work with the work of his Father in heaven.

Let me close by sharing with you a story from Keith Miller.

> Years ago an old evangelist gave me a picture of evangelising the world. He told me about a small town in France where there was a perfume factory that made lavender fragrance. At five o'clock in the evening, when the bell would ring and the factory day was over, the workers would all go home. And as they walked down their separate streets, the whole town would be permeated with the scent of lavender. In much the same way, when the people of God leave the church and go to our work and to our homes, the whole community should be permeated with the kind of love and caring we are absorbing from our life together in the church. The world will be permeated with the scent of love as we move into its streets from our times together.

My prayer for you as you finish this book is that this scent of love, which you've picked up from Jesus, will be obvious to everyone around you, so that you in your turn will be a link in the chain that brings other people to faith in Christ.

~

Sources

The quotation from Keith Miller is from his book *The Scent of Love* (Waco, Texas; Word Books; 1983), 157. It is used by personal permission of the author.

ABOUT THE AUTHOR

Tim Chesterton was born in England and moved to Canada at the age of seventeen. He has served for over forty years in full-time ministry with the Anglican Church of Canada, in Ontario, Saskatchewan, the Northwest Territories, and Alberta. He currently resides in Edmonton. He and his wife Marci have four adult children, and as of the time of writing they have two grandchildren. Tim enjoys writing and walking in the Saskatchewan River valley, and he can often be found playing guitar and singing traditional folk songs in the coffee shops of Edmonton.

Manufactured by Amazon.ca
Bolton, ON

34448704R00094